CONTINUOUS IMPROVEMENT *Without* CONTINUOUS STRESS

STRATEGIES FOR SCHOOL LEADERS

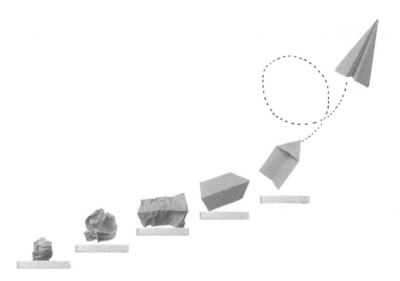

LESLI LAUGHTER

First Edition.
Paperback ISBN: 979-8-89185-063-7
Hardcover ISBN: 979-8-89185-064-4
Ebook ISBN: 979-8-89185-065-1
Library of Congress Number: 2024931111

hope*books
hopebooks.com

"In her book, *Continuous Improvement Without Continuous Stress*, Lesli Laughter shares a sequence of strategies that work together to demystify the school improvement process. She shares anecdotal examples making it clear that she has been an educational practitioner giving credibility to the steps she shares. The tools incorporated in each chapter serve as a guidepost helping school leaders to set a clear path to navigating data analysis and incorporating a comprehensive needs assessment while building a collaborative culture for school improvement. A must read for anyone looking to go beyond the status quo springboarding their school's transformation."

Dale K. Castro, Ed.D.
Complex Academic Officer
Hawai'i Department of Education

In *Continuous Improvement Without Continuous Stress*, Lesli Laughter offers school leaders fresh and clear guidelines for continuous improvement. While some planning models have strict formats and confusing vocabulary, Laughter explains the essential components of planning in a streamlined model that is easy to use. It also helps school leaders make sense of and strengthen existing school systems. What makes her book unique is that instead of simply describing what to do, she explains why. Her streamlined model makes strong connections between the root causes of problems and the actions developed to eliminate them. With tools and templates that save time, this is a book that every busy school leader needs to read."

Justin Richardson, Ed.D.
CEO
Waymaker Leadership Development

"Lesli's ability to transcend compliance to continuous improvement is evident in this masterpiece. This book guides school leaders on how to lead a school that gets results. Every school and district leader should use this book to ensure their schools are reaching the outcomes every student they serve deserves."

Matt Pope
Founder & CEO
EDpact

"This book is an indispensable resource for educators seeking to transform their improvement planning process and enrich the learning experiences for their students. The timelessness of quality planning is clearly mapped out by Lesli Laughter as she shows why schools must move from planning as a one time, beginning-of-school event to planning as an essential process for operating effective schools. From setting clear goals to analyzing outcomes, the book guides educators through steps that are both intuitive and effective for driving meaningful, positive change. Both novice and experienced school leaders will benefit from the descriptions, examples, and tools presented."

Kel Spradling
Vice President of Professional Learning
806 Technologies, Inc.

"All school leaders should read this book to affirm, adjust, or amplify their continuous improvement practices. The book will help them decide what to continue, what to start, and most importantly, what to abandon. This will be transformational for schools that see creating a needs assessment and developing the school plan as separate or loosely connected activities. Lesli not only masterfully and clearly defines the components of both needs assessment and plans, but also brings clarity to how they are deeply interconnected. Her continuous improvement structure, combined with storytelling and visuals, checks all the boxes of simple, effective, and practical processes for busy school leaders."

Cindy Gibson
Chief of Professional Learning
806 Technologies, Inc.

To school leaders everywhere,
past, present, and future.
You make the world a better place.

For my husband, Steve.
Always and forever!
You are my world.

For my sons, Ross and Clay.
For my mom, Sylvia.
No one cheered me on more than you.
Thank you for believing.

TABLE OF CONTENTS

INTRODUCTION

"How do you develop your school's continuous improvement plan?" I asked at a recent educator's conference. As I approached a middle school principal from Texas, I expected to hear about effective data analysis, innovative strategies, creative approaches, and student-centered goals. Instead, I was surprised to hear the principal's open admission, "I simply revise the dates in last year's plan, change a few things here and there, and then check it off my to-do list so I can get back to what I was hired to do—orchestrate the *real* plans for improving teaching and learning at my school." This sentiment is not uncommon. Many continuous improvement plans are jargon-filled documents created to meet federal funding requirements or district deadlines. They lack practical value for teachers, principals, and other school leaders. As an educator and continuous improvement specialist, I find this same scenario in schools all over the United States. So, my surprise wasn't about what she said, but her willingness to openly admit frustration. Continuous improvement planning can make an incredible difference in a school's growth. Unfortunately, state and federal laws that primarily focus on compliance plus the load of requirements in some districts have made it difficult for school leaders.

One issue with these plans is that they are not user-friendly for the people responsible for implementing them. Complicated spreadsheets or fill-in-the-blank Word documents may fulfill district-level requirements or state and federal laws, but they can make it difficult for school leaders to understand and apply the plans to their everyday work. I found this to be true in my own experience as an assistant superintendent. When preparing the district's continuous improvement plan for presentations to stakeholders and the board of trustees, I started with defeat, thinking, "Why bother?" I knew another thick document loaded with student achievement data, goals, objectives, and strategies was not beneficial to

1

anyone. The continuous improvement plan is meant to tell the district's story, identify strengths and needs, and outline strategies for improvement. However, the format was so cumbersome that it was difficult to piece a story together. I knew that the plan would meet compliance requirements, but it would have little impact on the continuous improvement work occurring throughout the district.

Even the process of developing the plan was cumbersome. The stakeholder committee entrusted with helping the district develop the continuous improvement plan—consisting of parents, school personnel, and community members—would review the previous year's plan, thick with acronyms, school jargon, too many initiatives, and legal requirements. They would study the most recent state assessment scores, comment positively on how hard everyone was working, revise a few dates, and then approve the document housed in an impressive, glossy binder. The district's continuous improvement plan would be excessive in size but low on practical value for the district's team of educators.

I was committed to finding a better way to plan. I wanted to generate a healthy urgency to create plans for students to learn and grow. The old planning process was no longer effective, and I knew that we needed to cut through ineffective practices and create a more practical, user-friendly approach. Dr. Douglas Reeves, the author of *Deep Change Leadership,* explains the problem this way:

> Too many educational leaders in the 21st century persist in strategic-planning models that were designed for 20th century challenges. The economic and public health challenges of 2020 only revealed the weaknesses in these outdated and ineffective change models. It should not require another crisis for leaders to seize the opportunity to apply new models of change leadership for the challenges that lie ahead. (Reeves 2021, 1)

Even though I was highly committed to changing our continuous improvement plan and implementation processes, I didn't know where to begin. My breakthrough in developing a new kind of plan occurred quite by accident one year later when I was once again working on the district's continuous improvement plan. It was a weekend and my oldest son, Ross, a software developer, was home visiting. He sensed my frustration while I was working, and he asked what I was doing. I showed him the cumbersome software program and terrible format that our district used to compile the district improvement plan.

It didn't take Ross long to understand the problem, and he offered to code a new software program for me. I described my dream for software that could support a robust needs assessment process designed to build upon the school's assets and identify the root causes of problems. The software would be used by multiple teams, comply with state and federal regulations, and prioritize the most important problems. This information would be used as the foundation for developing goals and strategies to address students' needs. I also requested components for the missing pieces in our current improvement plans, including easy tools for monitoring and evaluation. One of the main reasons continuous improvement planning often fails is that developing a plan is unproductive without pairing it with actions—implementation, progress monitoring, adjusting, and an end-of-year evaluation. After all, continuous improvement is about improving the *actions* of people. A plan is just words on paper unless you bring it to life through the beliefs, commitments, and actions of those involved.

My conversations with Ross continued over the next few months, and this marked the birth of Plan4Learning Continuous Improvement Software. We quickly implemented the new software in my school district, and it revolutionized the way continuous improvement planning occurred. Principals and central office administrators loved Plan4Learning's features and processes. Through informal conversations between educators, word spread to other school districts. It wasn't long before Ross was receiving calls from a rapidly growing number of school districts requesting to use the software. He never intended to start a company, but the software sold itself. Today, 806 Technologies has grown into a flourishing, nationwide company, with multiple software products and professional learning. I am privileged to serve as the company's Chief Academic Officer.

This book is not about Plan4Learning software or a marketing promotion for 806 Technologies. Telling my 806 Tech story explains why I have the opportunity and honor to work with hundreds of school districts and charter schools. For over a decade, my central focus has remained the same—to help schools and districts develop a core operating system for creating high-quality continuous improvement plans and the processes required for implementation, monitoring, and evaluation. When a school values this core operating system, continuous improvement is not an add-on; the entire school experience includes systemic growth. Conducting a self-analysis based on data and then implementing aligned actions with frequent checks for progress becomes a standard operation. Ideally, this continuous improvement core operating system would be evident throughout the district. But the reality is that it's often not. School leaders are usually eager to implement and build upon continuous improvement, but the weight of responsibilities and urgent demands push planning aside. The question I am most frequently asked is, "How can we do it?"

To start, schools need to shift their thinking about the way they see continuous improvement planning. Many districts see planning as simply completing a document (a task). Instead, we must understand continuous improvement planning (combined with implementation) as laying the groundwork for how we will operate our school. Planning then becomes a *process* that uses the document as a *tool* in school operations. To address the Texas principal's response, *real* planning begins with a culture that focuses on the school's vision. It collectively embraces the school's mission, strategically implements strategies aimed to support student growth, and regularly monitors the impact of the school's actions. Continuous improvement is more than a document. It includes processes and actions. It is improving how adults work and this is challenging. It requires active and dedicated effort.

Unfortunately, there are no easy solutions or quick-fix formulas that can guarantee success. However, this book presents many ideas that can help reduce the stress of planning and strengthen your school's continuous improvement processes. The ideas presented are based upon these continuous improvement principles:

1. Continuous improvement is a core operating system and not a program or event. It begins with a vivid vision. The mission creates urgency for educators to work smarter and get better every day so that students can achieve success.

2. A healthy school culture is critical for success. Schools where teachers and principals share responsibility for outcomes and build strong, trusting relationships will flourish. These schools demonstrate a growth mindset and celebrate each other's courage, creativity, and success. This is a school where continuous improvement can thrive.

3. A comprehensive needs assessment is critical. Identifying the school's strengths, critical needs, and the root causes of those needs before developing a plan of action is essential.

4. The plan of action which I label as the GPS (Goals, Performance objectives, and Strategies) must be clear, prioritized, and well-defined. The plan should consist of a few key goals, a small number of SMARTER performance objectives, and powerful BEST strategies. SMARTER and BEST characteristics are defined in Chapter 6.

5. Monitoring impact and adjusting actions when necessary are essential for continuous growth and improvement. Implementing a consistent cycle of status checks every 90 days keeps the school focused and greatly increases the school's rate of success.

6. A thorough evaluation at the end of each year is easy to do when monitoring occurs throughout the year. The evaluation can inform and enhance the next year's comprehensive needs assessment.

One of the most compelling things about continuous improvement planning is experiencing a school's strategically designed growth. When growth is by design, everyone benefits. We are undeniably in an era of constant change for education. To create the schools that students need, we can't sit back and operate in reactive mode. We must proactively design a plan for change, take action, and test our impact. True school transformation occurs because of a plan, not by chance. It is exciting to think about how continuous improvement planning can benefit students and teachers. Change is coming! Let's plan for it.

Chapter 1

VISION –
WHY DREAMS MATTER

> *"Dream no small dreams for they have no power to move the hearts of men."*
> *Johann Wolfgang von Goethe*

Goethe's words are a powerful reminder of the importance of having a bold and inspiring vision. A vision statement is not just a collection of words; it is an influential tool that should ignite passion. You can't become what you don't see. Whether you are a superintendent, a principal, or other school leader seeking to make a meaningful impact in your school community, embracing a captivating vision is essential to achieving your goals. Every great achievement begins with a vision. From world-changing inventions to personal triumphs, the ability to picture future goals has been the driving force behind some of humanity's most remarkable accomplishments. A school's vision should be no less. It should stir all those who interact with the school and create a sense of urgency to be fully committed—to achieve and do more. It is a broad, aspirational description of what the school will deliver when everything in the world is right. A compelling vision can inspire and motivate the entire school community. It gives stakeholders a clear picture of what the school desires to become and the impact it will have. Vision unites people to work together toward a bold, prosperous future—where vision becomes destiny.

THE WHAT AND WHY OF VISION

The school's vision plays a key role in fostering a culture of excellence and continuous improvement. A common way to develop the school's vision is through a collaborative process that involves a variety of stakeholders, including administrators, teachers, parents, students, and community members. To be effective, the process must be inclusive and respectful of multiple ideas and perspectives. This is not a one-time event. Often the same vision stays in place for years. However, our world innovates and changes at breakneck speed. To stay relevant, schools must regularly review and revise their vision for the future. A good time to do this is prior to the beginning of a new school year's planning cycle. Carve out some time to bring people together to reflect on the current state of the school and dream about the future. How will your school change the world?

The vision explains why you do what you do (your inspiration), the motivation behind what you do (what keeps you going), and the energy it takes to sustain the inspiration and motivation over time (future-based). When school teams are inspired, motivated, and can view a better future ahead, they are emboldened to carry out the school's mission. (We will explore mission statements in the next chapter.) Ideally, this would be the only item on the agenda. Unlocking the power of visionary dreams and turning them into a passion for the future is a process that shouldn't be rushed.

Vision and mission are often grouped together. You see them in strategic plans, school improvement plans, and other important school documents. While schools need both, neither one is typically used well. Vision and mission have value. They can be more than old, dusty statements that are a muddled heap of goals, values, and strategies.

One of the most convincing values is that without a clear vision, a school can easily be thrown off track. Achieving goals is hard. Think about the last time you set a personal goal. Many of us experience strong commitment at the beginning but then abandon the goal after just a few weeks. So many distractions can get in the way of success. As a school leader, are you constantly bombarded with ideas for improvement from vendors, central office administration, parents, teachers, and the community? Everyone has a solution. Simplicity is strained because of more—more options, more complexity, more uncertainty. Even with "more" flooding into our daily lives, schools are expected to make agile and rapid decisions. Demands for customization and personalization in education are solidly here to stay, making it imperative for educators to have a strong plan of action anchored by a clearly defined vision for success.

So, we return to our central question: How do we define the word *vision* in a school context? The vision or purpose is the north star that crystallizes educators' aspirations for students. It is a passionate description of what education will be like when the school moves beyond state exams and accountability standards. A vision describes a school where stakeholders' hopes and dreams for children are fulfilled. Anne Conzemius and Jan O'Neill, authors of *The Handbook for SMART School Teams*, explain:

> A vision is a compelling picture of a preferred future that motivates us to act. Some refer to vision as a hope or a dream. But vision is more than that. It might start as a hope or a dream, but it doesn't become a vision until there is some specificity about what that dream will look like in reality. What distinguishes a dream from a vision is the detail of the vision in action, something people can see or envision themselves doing. That is what makes a vision compelling. That is why vision motivates us to act—sometimes in ways that are very different than we ever would have imagined. (2014, 239)

In short, your school's vision explains why your school exists. Vision is the expected destiny for students. Without it, the mission—which gives meaning to the daily work—will not thrive in the long run.

WHOSE VISION?

It was October and I had been hired to be the principal of a brand new school—not just a new school, but a brand new concept. The intermediate school concept was to move sixth and seventh grades into a two-grade school that served as a bridge between elementary school and junior high.

Throughout the fall before the school opened, I met with parents, teachers and staff, students from the current elementary schools and from the junior high to explain the new concept and build support for the school. I was enthusiastic about the new opportunity, but I soon discovered that I seemed to be standing alone in my excitement. Nearly every idea about the new intermediate school concept was met with resistance to change.

We had an approach that included parents, teachers, and students in helping design the new school concept. I did my best to be a "good listener." Despite all this, it just wasn't working. Teachers liked where they were and didn't want to change schools. Parents worried over new bus schedules, routines, and course requirements. Rising sixth grade students were apprehensive because they were ready to go to junior high. They were afraid the new school would feel more elementary. Rising seventh grade students who were already in junior high felt like it was a step backwards. I spent a tremendous amount of time trying to persuade people to use their concerns to help create an ideal setting, but I was getting nowhere.

It would have been easy to give up.

Instead, I met with my new assistant principal and a small core of teacher leaders. Together, we changed the tactic. In the second round of meetings, we discarded our ask-a-question approach. We started the meetings with stories and pictures of other innovative schools—inside and outside the district. We talked about the characteristics of sixth and seventh graders and formed small groups to talk about structures to fit their developmental needs. We brainstormed what classes should be offered. How would the school be designed? What about the ideal schedule? How would we establish a culture appropriate for students? What about athletics? Nothing was off the table.

Next, we chose adjectives to describe these ideal conversations of what could be. After writing the adjectives down, we grouped them by like words—similar to a keyword list used in search engine optimization.

Then, our stakeholders had the opportunity to add additional words and to create assertions about the kind of school they envisioned.

The result? We saw people become energized. Teachers, parents, and students from different schools were now interacting together, fueling the shared passion for what the new school could look like. Attendance at our planning meetings grew and talk turned from complaints to contributions. People shared, embraced, and celebrated their hopes and dreams for the new school. The school opened with a unique structure built upon the support of the community, a passionate staff, and happy students. This is what a vision can do.

REFRESH YOUR SCHOOL'S VISION

A school's vision can change over time, so it is important to provide time for stakeholders to revisit and revise the vision every couple of years or any time a big change occurs. Mike Myatt, a leadership advisor to Fortune 500 companies, says that a vision and mission work in tandem, but they are not interchangeable and should never be viewed as static. In his N2Growth blog he writes, "It's important to note that both vision and mission should be viewed as variables and not constants. What I mean by this is both the vision and mission need to be kept fresh and relevant. If either your vision or mission becomes outdated and irrelevant, so too will your business." (Myatt n.d.)

Is it time for a vision refresh? What will you communicate in your vision statement? This section helps you put feet to your school's future by passionately describing your school's destination. Before you get started, remember that a vision should:

- **Be unique to your school.** A vision that declares your school will be an "environment of educational excellence" sounds just like every other school. It's not unique. What makes your school different? What drives *your* community's passion? Take some time and really think this through. Brainstorm with multiple stakeholder groups. Remember, a tired, dusty vision doesn't create excitement for the future.

- **Energize and inspire your team.** If visitors to your school read the vision and think it sounds similar to one found in the lobby of a hotel or on the first floor of their office building, it isn't right for your school. Your vision should infuse energy into conversations about teaching and learning. This is the part where you get to ask your team to stretch to the furthest edges of their imaginations. What monumentally grand plans do they want to pursue? What will their magnificent future school be like? The conversations that follow will likely bring your vision into sharper view.

- **Exclude action-oriented daily to-do items that your school must do anyway.** Forget the day-to-day inner workings of your school or district: try to exclude the parts you know you must do, such as safety protocols and meeting state standards. These are baseline tasks that don't inspire. Your vision should be one sentence that *reflects* a long-term, future-oriented "best of" description of results and impact that keeps your team wholeheartedly fired up and engaged in the work (the mission).

WHY VISION MATTERS

What happened when our team of school leaders changed tactics to build excitement and support for the new school? The message we had to share was received in a totally different way. Attitudes changed and mindset shifted. Constructive collaboration took over and the community enthusiastically embraced the concept of an intermediate school.

Vision brings energy to the table. And that is exactly what happened.

The community was eager for the new school to open once they had collective ownership over the vision. Their dreams and desires were focused into one clearly defined picture for the future. And from day one, the new school was a success.

Sometimes, we need to get out of our own way. We need to look at problems differently, ask new questions, and invite new stakeholders to the table. Developing a great vision doesn't happen overnight, and it involves multiple perspectives; it takes work.

But as the Cheshire Cat advises in one of my favorite books, *Alice in Wonderland*, you've got to keep the why behind the work at the forefront of your mind. At one point, Alice stops and asks the Cheshire Cat which way to go. He, in turn, asks her where she wants to go. When she says that she doesn't know, the Cheshire Cat concludes that it doesn't matter which road she chooses then.

We can't be like Alice. We must specifically know where we are heading. Students depend on us to prepare them for a world that doesn't yet exist.

Once you have your school's vision in place, Figure 1.1 provides ideas for how you can use it.

Figure 1.1 Vision as a Tool

USING THE VISION AS A TOOL

 EXPLAIN IT

Begin the school year with a thoughtful review of the school's vision. Ask the staff to get into groups of 5-6 people. Have them search for quotes about vision on the Internet through their phones. Have each group select one quote and present it to the entire staff. When presenting the quote, the group should explain why they chose that one and how it relates to the school vision.

 FIND PERSPECTIVE

Take a few minutes to brainstorm the similarities and differences between working in a department store and working in a school. Give the staff 2-3 minutes to reflect how they work with "customers" (students and families) at school. Have a few people share their thoughts and how they align with the school's vision.

 UNITE WITH IT

Seek commitment. Talk about the near future and distant future perspectives. Have staff, families, and students sign a pledge to be "all in" with the vision. Line the hallways with pledge cards. Redo this at the beginning of each school year.

 CLARIFY THE WHY

When the work gets tough or when considering an initiative that is a major shift in operating procedures or instructions, encourage others to recommit to the vision before making changes.

 REPEAT, REPEAT, REPEAT

Be able to explain the vision in different words for students, families, staff and community. Add it as your desktop background. Create laptop stickers. Use it in the footer of your emails. Include it at the beginning of presentations. Put it in places around your desk so you will be reminded to remind others.

STRESS RELIEF: REVISE YOUR VISION

1. The first step to revise your school's vision is to consider these questions with a core team of school leaders.

   a. If we had no barriers, what is the most magnificent education we could provide for our students? What are our greatest hopes and dreams for students? Create a list of ideas.

   b. Considering the ideas above, what impact do we want our school to have?

   c. What do families, students, and staff value most? What are our shared values?

   d. Consider the ideas generated by the three questions above. If we could talk about anything for hours, as it relates to making our school better, what would that be? (This will likely encompass more than one topic. That's encouraged; write everything down.)

      • Are there specific areas of inspiration that you see when you look at other districts, schools, or innovative ideas?

      • As you think about our changing world and what students will need to thrive, which ideas and topics excite you enough to work toward them day after day?

      • Can we narrow our list to two or three ideas that most inspire us about future education?

   e. Debrief the process with your team. What questions were easy to answer? Were any of the questions confusing? What background information will the group need in order to successfully answer the questions? How can this process best be facilitated with a larger group of people?

   f. Discuss steps 2 and 3 below and how they can best be facilitated in a large group of stakeholders.

2. The next step is to invite a more representative group of stakeholders to go through the same exercise. This time, add a larger group of staff members and include families and community members. High schools may want to include students. Lead the group through the same questions above. Then, ask:

   a. Do these two or three ideas represent the most magnificent education that we want to provide for our students?

   b. Do these ideas create a springboard for crafting a mission to easily go alongside them?

   c. Do these represent innovative thinking that goes beyond what the school currently offers? Can we envision this "ideal" becoming the norm in the future?

3. Step three is to craft the ideas into a simple, concise, easy-to-remember statement. Then check for these:

   a. Does the vision clearly describe *what* the school wants to accomplish?

   b. Does it explain *why* this matters?

   c. Is it free from educational jargon and excessive wordiness?

   d. Is it compelling enough that we will be willing to fight through barriers and obstacles to see it come to fruition?

Chapter 2

MISSION AND
PURPOSEFUL BEHAVIOR

> *"Vision sees the stars; mission carves the path to reach them.*
> *Vision without a purposeful mission is a ship without*
> *a compass, drifting aimlessly in the sea of aspirations."*
> *Aloo Denish Obiero*

What does it mean when you are "on a mission?" Typically, that means you are driven by a strong sense of purpose or a goal that you are actively working toward. Being on a mission implies that you are committed to achieving a specific outcome, often at all costs. You are willing to make sacrifices or take risks to make it happen.

Your school has a mission that explains the drive and purpose of the work so that the school can achieve its vision. A school's mission is different from the business world because schools focus on people and not products. Some of the most common ways schools are evaluated for success are frustrating for educators because the business-like characteristics don't match what schools need. For example, the bottom line for most businesses is profit. They want the best return on investment by selling all their goods in the shortest time possible, for the highest price possible, while incurring the lowest production costs. Doesn't that sound very similar to the accountability placed on schools? In only thirteen years and while appropriately incurring the available funds, schools will graduate the largest possible number of students who pass required exams and meet the requirements for attendance, career, college, or military readiness. While these characteristics may be important, would any superintendent tell you *that* is their district's mission? I doubt it. A quality education for children is the "product" schools want to produce. Because providing an education for human beings is very different from producing a widget in a factory, schools can't always strictly embrace business structures without modifications. Let's take this a step further.

Have you ever been in a job interview where the interviewer grilled you about the proficiency scores of the schools you attended? Or did you have to provide the accountability rating of your high school when applying for a teaching or administrative position in your district?

Probably not.

Employers are much more interested in your personal skills and qualifications than the rankings or ratings of your alma mater. Of course, school rankings and accountability ratings are important and have their place. They provide a measure of how well schools are meeting state and federal standards. But what really drives the actions for a school's success?

The answer lies in its mission. What is a school's mission? If you think of the vision as an exquisite work of art painted on a canvas, the mission is the brushstrokes that bring that canvas to life. The mission needs a future-focused vision of the finished masterpiece. But, the mission is the action needed to complete the artwork. Mission is like consistently dipping the brush in paint and meticulously crafting the strokes to create the masterpiece. The mission gives meaning to your work. When we know what we want to create (the vision), we can be better at choosing how we will work and what work we choose to do (the mission). Just like owning a canvas doesn't make someone an accomplished artist, having a mission statement doesn't mean a school has a mission. Writing one to simply post on the website is useless. Mission is about how you can contribute to making the school better. It describes what you commit to do and how you intend to act. The purpose of a mission is to inspire and direct committed actions—every day.

WHY IS MISSION IMPORTANT?

Everyone needs a purpose. In his book, *Future Driven*, David Geurin, principal at Bolivar High School in Bolivar, Missouri, says, "If students graduate with a diploma, but without a sense of mission or purpose, we are falling short in our mission and purpose. Education is bigger than the standards we have to teach. Education is learning more about who you are and how you contribute to making the world a better place." (2017, 180) To accomplish this, educators must model the mission every day and provide opportunities for students to embrace the mission for their work. Geurin continues, "School leaders must focus on clarifying a shared sense of mission that is truly a mission and not focused on test results." (2017, 29) If we can establish a school culture that believes everyone has a responsibility to contribute to make the school a better place, implementing continuous improvement is easy. The next chapter will further describe how to build a culture that supports this belief.

A mission statement on a piece of paper or printed on a plaque hanging on the wall doesn't change a school's path. Human beings do. As educators, we are in the business of changing lives, and thus, changing the world. So, our ability to own the mission is crucial. Often when a school is ready to conduct a needs assessment and build a plan of action to address needs, no thought is given to the mission. This is a mistake. The mission is what motivates people to create and implement an innovative plan to improve. It provides a sense of direction, focus, and meaning to the work. It also supports when things get challenging as schools often face obstacles, setbacks, and difficult choices as they engage in continuous improvement.

The beginning of a new school year is always exciting for me. Every year I feel like I need to go buy new school supplies. After all, who doesn't love a set of new highlighters and pens? As a principal, another exciting part of the new year was hiring new first-year teachers and getting to know them. Their enthusiasm and excitement bubbles over into everything they do. They can't wait to get started. One example of how much mission matters is in a story about a first-year teacher named Sara.

At the beginning of the year, Sara's joy was contagious. She smiled ear-to-ear, and it was obvious that she loved her job. School started well, and Sara quickly moved into a good routine. However, as time progressed, things began to unravel. Sara slowly lost her joy. She found that teaching takes high levels of energy everyday, and some days can be really difficult. As the weeks rolled by, Sara was just barely making it from day to day. She did her job, but fell into an exhausted routine of minimally managing her daily tasks. She longed for the last bell of the day and rarely participated in anything extra. In October, our school hosted a math carnival at night. Students were asked to bring at least one adult with them to have some fun with numbers. As the event was about to begin, I noticed Sara's room was dark. No one had seen her, and when she didn't answer her phone, I called her husband. That phone call revealed a big surprise. He told me that Sara wouldn't be there that night or the next day. He said Sara's teaching days were over, and she wouldn't be returning to school—ever. Following years of work to obtain her degree, Sara was ready to quit after just a few weeks. Sara had lost all purpose and drive for teaching. She needed a new focus, a compelling driving force—a mission! The good news is that Sara's story didn't end there. By assigning Sara a mentor and providing academic coaching, Sara stayed and eventually became a strong teacher and school leader.

Now, it would be ridiculous to think that developing and implementing a school mission is all it takes to support and retain first-year teachers. But, this unfortunate event was a wake-up call for me. I knew that a strong sense of mission in a school strengthens the culture and builds community. When people share the same mission, they work together and support each other. If Sara was ready to quit in October, I had some work to do.

You've heard it said that today is not a dress rehearsal and that is true. Every day at school is "the live show," and there's no time to waste. When your school mission is based upon a bold, dream-filled vision, it can help build a strong, united culture among teachers and staff. If your vision is strong and your mission isn't contributing to cultural growth, maybe it's time for a refresh. Investigate when the mission was created. If it has been more than three years, bring the mission before the staff for review. Look deeply at the words and the meaning behind them. Ask someone new to the school to describe what they think it means. To succeed with the mission, your school must act in single-minded devotion toward the vision. If the mission is not a clear, how-to statement that boldly asserts expectations for behavior, then start the revision process. A revised mission statement can strengthen the current stakeholders' commitment to achieving the school's vision.

Mahatma Gandhi is credited with this familiar quote, "A small body of determined spirits fired by an unquenchable faith in their mission can alter the course of human history." A powerful mission fires up those "determined spirits." Do you feel energized when you read your school's mission? Does it foster and promote the success of others? Creating a mission does nothing to improve learning without every staff member and stakeholder committing to action. Is it time to revise your mission? If so, let's get started.

QUESTIONS TO ASK *BEFORE* YOU REFINE YOUR SCHOOL'S MISSION

Begin with a small circle of school leaders. Building, as Gandhi said, "a small body of determined spirits" is critical before providing opportunities for all staff members to participate in a revision of the mission. With this small team, use these targeted questions to begin the revision conversations:

1. What does it mean to be "on mission" to see our vision fulfilled?

2. What would be possible if all of us are operating at our very best? What would that look like?

3. What are we willing to do every day (our mission) to transform the school's vision into our students' destiny?

4. What does our mission need to say that reflects our commitment and a sense of urgency?

5. How will we hold one another accountable to do the right-now, everyday things that our mission requires?

In some schools, conversations about improvement focus on topics such as programs to implement, how to teach certain concepts, or professional learning. These conversations are the daily work and usually target one grade level or one subject area. These are too detailed and narrow to be included in the mission. You may have to guide teachers to step outside the targeted daily work and view the entire school at once, seeing the school from the same perspective as a drone hovering overhead. Thinking about daily improvement actions from a drone's perspective promotes a higher-level conversation. This conversation is about how everyone will work in concert together, each from his or her personalized role, to make the school operate effectively. This is a mission.

With your small group of school leaders, create a draft mission statement. Then, plan similar conversations with the rest of the staff. It is helpful to continue with small groups such as grade levels or departments to encourage deeper conversations. When the staff has completed their work on the draft mission, give families and community members opportunities to submit their feedback. Continue to refine until your staff and stakeholders can embrace the statement.

The format for the mission is flexible. A shorter length with plain language is always best, but the most important factor is meaning. The mission is present-based, actionable, and contributes to educators' work through promises of what the school will provide for children every day. Gaining commitment from many stakeholders in a variety of roles makes the mission work. Like a brick house that is laid one brick at a time, each person needs to own his or her brick and be willing to lay that brick so that a collective future is attainable. This takes time, but building your mission right will pay off when it is time for implementation. This process sets the groundwork for implementing continuous improvement as a core operating function of the school.

QUESTIONS TO ASK *WHILE* YOU REVISE YOUR MISSION

1. What actions and commitments will it take today to move closer to the vision right now?

2. What are the non-negotiables?

3. What do we pledge to do for our students every day?

4. How can we help each other follow through on these commitments?

5. Is the mission well-written? Is it too vague or too narrow? Is it in clear language free from educational jargon?

A mission statement is typically one or two sentences, usually a little longer than the vision statement. But each statement is uniquely created, so don't let these guidelines limit your thinking. Below are three examples of vision and mission statements retrieved from the school districts' websites. I have worked with all three districts and know they have a clear vision of where they are going with explicit direction on how to get there. See if you can find the exemplary traits for a mission and identify how the vision statement drives it.

The School District of Pickens County in Easley, South Carolina, has this future-focused vision: "The vision of the School District of Pickens County is to *empower* each student for college, career, and life success." Their mission states, "The mission of the School District of Pickens County is to *engage* each student today to RISE to tomorrow's potential." RISE is an acronym for the school district's core values of respect, innovation, service and excellence.

The vision for Prosper Independent School District in Prosper, Texas, is, "Grounded by Tradition, Soaring to New Beginnings." To achieve that vision, the school district developed this mission: "The mission of PISD is to develop and graduate motivated, academically prepared individuals with the strength of character to make contributions to a rapidly changing society through an educational system that maintains high expectations, provides quality instruction and establishes a safe, orderly learning environment in the community that lives its name."

Prince William County Public Schools in Manassas, Virginia, adopted this vision: "Every student will graduate on time with the knowledge, skills, and habits of mind necessary to create a thriving future for themselves and their community." Their mission is in three statements:

- We serve as trusted partners in education with our students, families, and community.

- We prepare our students to be critical thinkers, responsible digital citizens, innovators and visionaries, resilient individuals, and global collaborators.

- We commit to inclusive practices and equity with an expectation of excellence from every student and employee every day.

MULTIPLE MISSION STATEMENTS

Some schools may find it beneficial to have each department, grade level, stakeholder group, or any other division in the school develop their own mission statement based upon the school's vision statement. Connie Hamilton, Joseph Jones, and T.J. Vari explain this variation in their book, *7 Mindshifts for School Leaders*, "Every division of the school should have a mission statement, and they all start the same way: 'The mission of the (insert school division) is to uphold the vision of our school by...' and the rest of the statement includes what the department, committee, or team actually should do in practice." (2023, 111-112)

Here are examples of department mission statements based upon a school district's vision statement: The vision of our school is to prepare students to be globally competitive and highly productive citizens.

1. The mission of the math department is to uphold the vision of our school by learning to communicate mathematically and becoming mathematical problem solvers.

2. The mission of the athletics department is to uphold the vision of our school by emphasizing the importance of physical activity as part of a daily, life-long habit that promotes health and wellness.

3. The mission of the PTO is to uphold the vision of our school by complementing the curriculum with additional opportunities for families, teachers, and students to learn, socialize, communicate and grow.

Hamilton, Jones and Vari state that while the missions of various departments sound disconnected, they each produce a unique pathway toward accomplishing the vision that can be measured. They also open the doors for a new kind of accountability. "Additionally, the establishment of statements of this kind at the committee and department level provokes a new kind of accountability regarding what each committee needs to accomplish as a team and the work involved to achieve their mission." (2023, 112)

CORE VALUES

A logical next step after revising the mission is to review the school's core values, which are sometimes called collective commitments. Core values are fundamental principles that guide a school's behavior and decision-making processes. They are often deeply ingrained and typically enduring, serving as a constant reference point for making judgments and responding to situations that arise. Examples of core values include honesty, integrity, respect, responsibility, teamwork, excellence, and innovation. These values are considered essential to the school's success and are therefore emphasized and upheld through practices and policies.

Core values are a part of the school culture, but they are more than that. Core values set the standard for the foundational operating system of a school. They springboard from the mission and provide further details about the school's expectations for behavior. For example, during a discussion to update or revise the mission someone might recommend that always putting children first should be included. If that statement doesn't fit with the mission's wording, it then becomes a candidate for the school's core values.

Highland Park High School in Saint Paul, Minnesota, uses their core values as the standard for how the adults at school are expected to behave. The principal, Dr. Winston Tucker, says they haven't changed much over the last 10 years, but they are reviewed yearly. Since they were created by the staff, Highland Park titles their core values as Collective Commitments. Dr. Tucker says that keeping their Collective Commitments at the forefront of everything they do is essential. When they select professional learning, they look to see if the content aligns with them. Using the Collective Commitments helps the staff see why certain mandates are required. Dr. Tucker explains that "when staff understands why we ask them to do something, they are much more likely to embrace it. Collective Commitments helps the staff have a voice." See Highland Park's Collective Commitments in Figure 2.1

Figure 2.1 Highland Park High School's Collective Commitments

COLLECTIVE
Commitments

✓ Be intentional about connecting learning and curriculum to students' lives.

✓ Create a positive environment where relationships matter.

✓ Work collaboratively to align curriculum that is relevant, rigorous, and engaging.

✓ Be culturally and racially proficient.

✓ Communicate professionally and consistently with each other, students, and families.

✓ Be committed to continuous learning and professional learning.

Courtesy of Dr. Winston Tucker, principal
Highland Park High School
Saint Paul, Minnesota

The Profile of an Educator is another format that some schools use to document the qualities they value in their employees. Figure 2.2 below provides an example. While core values, collective commitments, and a Profile of an Educator may look different on paper, all three contain a similar purpose—to define the qualities, characteristics, and competencies desired and valued by all educators in the district.

Figure 2.2 Profile of a Future-Ready Educator

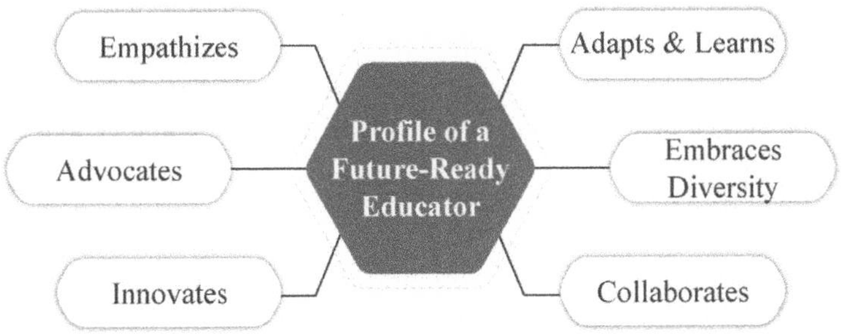

CORE VALUES IN ACTION

At my new intermediate school, we started with our mission to create our core values. The entire staff agreed to uphold these values because they further explained our mission and supported our vision. One of those values was to create a learning environment that allowed students to explore options to find their own strengths and abilities. Our core values helped us stay true to this new school design and our mission. Here's what happened:

Students were given opportunities to explore and experience a variety of courses through an elective wheel that changed every nine weeks. We wanted students to begin making decisions about what they liked and didn't like before committing to semester-long or year-long courses in junior high and high school. In our new school, we committed to making exploration a low-stakes process that was accessible to all.

During our first year, we had twelve 7th grade cheerleaders who had tried out the year before when they had been in sixth grade at the old junior high. We honored that selection process. They cheered just as they would have in a junior high setting. However, when the next year was rolling into view, we used our mission and core values as part of the evaluation process.

The cheerleading sponsor asked me to provide a date when rising seventh-grade students could try out for cheerleading. Together, we reviewed the successes and challenges of the year and reflected closely on one core value. Did this tryout—and the way it had always been done at the junior high level—fit our core value where *all* students would have the opportunity to explore? In the creation of our core values, our staff had promised that we would provide exploratory learning opportunities so that students could better develop their interests and talents.

Ultimately, we decided to still hold tryouts. However, we added something new. Any student who was willing to try out in front of the entire student body would be selected for the seventh-grade cheerleading squad. Because this mindset of allowing everyone to participate was so pervasive in our mission, it meant that we had to be willing to be different.

This also applied to football, basketball, volleyball, etc. Each sport had multiple teams, and there were plenty of opportunities for anyone who wanted to cheer to try it out. We received plenty of questioning looks when we traveled to other schools in the region. But we held strong with our commitment to allow students to explore and try new things. The feedback from our students and families was positive and appreciative.

STRESS RELIEF: THE POWER OF USING THE MISSION AS A TOOL

Reflect on your school's mission and think about ways to bring it more to life. This is not about adding another task on your to do list. The mission aligns behavior. It creates a sense of urgency and accountability for everyone to do their very best because the school year is short and every day matters. Pledging to uphold the mission and core values helps solidify continuous improvement as a fundamental operating process.

That's what this book is all about—continuous improvement. The entire continuous improvement planning cycle can be seen in Figure 2.3. Notice how the mission encircles all other components. The mission is the frame that holds all the pieces together. We'll learn about each of the components in the following chapters.

Figure 2.3 Continuous Improvement Planning Components

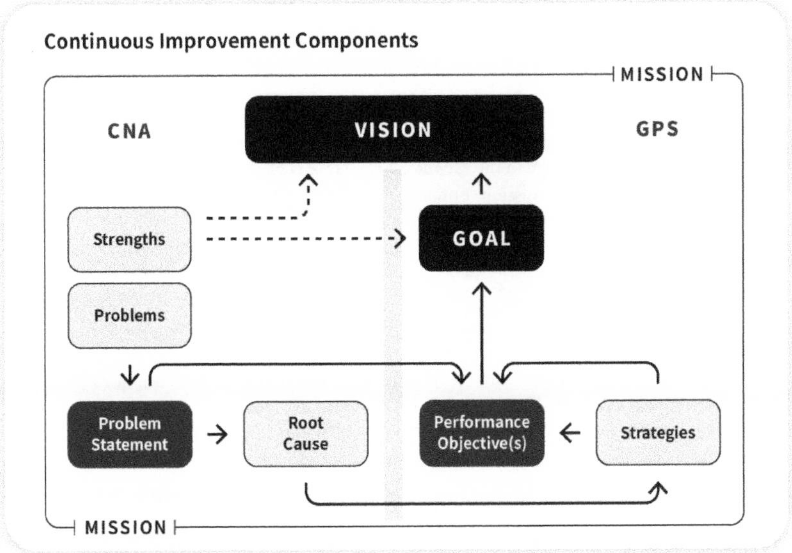

Continuous Improvement Components

CNA	VISION	GPS

Strengths ----→ GOAL

Problems

| Problem Statement | → | Root Cause | | Performance Objective(s) | ← | Strategies |

MISSION

Developing the school's mission is the easy part. Actually using it as a natural part of your school's operations may take some thought at first, but with consistency you can reap the benefits. Figure 2.4 below provides ideas that can help.

Figure 2.4 Thriving with the Mission

THRIVING WITH THE MISSION

BE ALL IN

Begin the school year with a thoughtful review of the school's mission. Ask questions like these: Does the mission reflect our collective beliefs about how we will work every day? Will this behavior help us achieve our vision? Does this mission still energize us? Can we commit to this as our school's urgent call to action for teaching and learning? Can you embrace what the mission says? Lay a rope on the floor or make a masking tape line. Ask those who can commit to the mission to physically cross the line and be ALL IN. Then, celebrate!

FRAME IT

Write the school's mission on a large piece of paper and add a date at the bottom. Ask and discuss the same questions listed in the activity above. Have each staff member sign the paper indicating commitment to the mission. Frame the page and display it in a location where students, families, and other stakeholders can readily see it. Repeat this activity at the beginning of each new year as a commitment to the implement the mission in order to achieve the vision.

ALIGN DECISIONS

When considering major decisions, first review the mission and core values. Then discuss these questions: How does this decision align with our school's mission? Will any part of this decision decelerate our mission? Does this decision conflict with any of our core values?

SETTLE CONFLICT

When conflicting opinions arise, focus on the mission. Determine which opinion better aligns. If the answer cannot be determined, review the core values to determine a process to reach a solution. Often the mission and core values can be used to help people self-monitor. Reviewing them identifies unwanted behaviors and describes behaviors that are valued and expected.

REPEAT, REPEAT, REPEAT

Explain how the mission creates a healthy urgency for actions that move people toward the vision. Encourage staff, families, and community members to embrace and respect the mission as a way to collectively support all students.

Chapter 3

CULTURE – THE SECRET SAUCE

> *"We need to shift from a teaching culture to a learning culture where we take risks and learn from mistakes. What we really want is for everyone to arrive at work as a learner."*
> Connie Hamilton, Joseph Jones, and T.J. Vari

We are shaped not only by our beliefs and values but also by the beliefs and values of those around us. Moments of observation, collaboration, and even confrontation all create conditions that factor in how a school's culture evolves. What does culture have to do with continuous improvement? Everything! Culture influences the way a school operates, and continuous improvement is an operating system.

When was the last time you heard the words culture and data in the same conversation? Not often, if ever, right? Bring up the idea of having a data-focused culture to support continuous improvement in schools and you are likely to stir differing opinions. Some school leaders may be puzzled because they see data analysis as an event stemming from compliance requirements. Their thinking is that data doesn't play a role in a school's culture. They only look at their data together as a school when they examine the state assessment results to predict the school's latest accountability ratings or compile a mandatory improvement plan. Schools with an unhealthy culture may define a data-focus as the lack of trust in teachers' professional judgment. They feel data is used as a snare to ensure teachers are teaching the right curricula or to box teachers in and reduce their ability to customize instructional design.

A focus on data doesn't have to be negative. In fact, many schools value the importance of data in a school culture. When trust abounds and core values exist, data analysis results in insights that complement, rather than undermine, professional judgment. School leaders who have been empowered to take charge of their own learning and help the school grow use data as a foundation for decision making. Teachers and principals study data together on a regular basis. They celebrate growth and figure out what is working and what isn't. They don't pit one teacher against another. Everyone learns together, and the success of one becomes the success of all. In schools like this, principals and teachers don't need to wait for outside auditors, accountability ratings or other measures to take action. With a strong data culture, school leaders have everything needed to monitor and accelerate their school's growth.

Implementing the practice of using systemic data doesn't occur spontaneously. You can't just wave a wand and expect it to happen. It involves the regular and collaborative utilization of data across the school to inform decisions aimed at enhancing student outcomes. It means collecting data before making changes in programs, instructions, and processes. This process takes time and plenty of training to implement. It requires consistent and intentional effort from school leaders. Building a culture of consistent data use is not easy, but it is worth it.

DATA-FOCUSED CULTURE

So how do schools establish a data-focused culture? The first thing to know is that changing the school's culture is vastly different from changing the math program or the master schedule. So give yourself some grace and don't expect a total transformation in just a few short weeks. Changing a school's culture typically occurs in small steps with small wins. The most important thing is to have a plan. Luckily, there is a great model to follow. In 2015, Nancy Gerzon and Sarah Guckenburg developed "A Toolkit for a Workshop on Building a Culture of Data Use." The toolkit is published by the Institute of Education Sciences (IES). IES is the part of the US Department of Education that provides research, evaluation, and statistics. The nonpartisan Toolkit is free (do a quick Internet search to find it) and has been field tested for success. It contains a facilitator's guide, a slide deck, and participant handouts. The Toolkit defines several assumptions that relate to developing a culture of data use. A great place to start with a culture reset is with an examination of your own personal beliefs about the following assumptions listed in the Toolkit:

- There is a tension between compliance-driven data use and inquiry-based data use. When teams examine data on a specific instructional issue and take time to explore multiple ways to solve the issue, their work is inquiry-based data use. Compare that with teams examining data on a specific instructional issue and counting to see how many more correct answers will push the school up to the next accountability rating. That is compliance-driven data use. When you find schools that are highly driven by accountability, those same schools almost always struggle to create a safe environment to explore and effectively use data.

- The goal of having a data-using culture is that everybody's practice improves.

- Interpreting evidence is not a solo act. Meaning comes from how a variety of individuals at different levels of the education system understand and make sense of data.

- Evidence informs professional judgment; it does not replace professional judgment. Recognize teachers' wealth of tacit knowledge as a starting point.

- Data do not, by themselves, lead to improvement.

- Educators need professional learning opportunities on instructional decision-making that considers the role of data.

- A culture of data use is built only when you set up the structures and practices, not the other way around.

- The context, the setting, and the environment in which data are delivered all matter.

- Personnel in effective data-using cultures use data in the course of their work, not in addition to their regular work.

- It is essential for educators at all levels of the education system to build multiple fluencies regarding data use. This is a key underpinning of a data-using culture. (2015, 22)

After your own self-reflection, use these bulleted statements to begin building or strengthening your school's culture. Start by leading conversations around the interpretation of each bullet above. Take time to reflect, discuss, and recognize the meaning of each statement. Do people at your school agree with these? What barriers need to be removed for people to agree?

CLIMATE AND CULTURE

Take a step back from culture and analyze the school's climate. What is the difference between culture and climate? "Climate is how people feel in the school, and culture is a deeper sense of how they act in a school." (Kane et al. 2016, 2) If we want teachers to work collaboratively as a team, they need a climate that is warm and accepting, inviting their input. Adjusting the climate is the first step to strengthening the culture because climate is perception-based. There are easy ways to help with climate. Start by asking people how they feel, but don't get trapped into thinking it is your responsibility to make them feel happy or good. It's not your responsibility, but understanding their perceptions is important. Also, observe interactions between various groups. This includes students and families. Watching the way people interact together can help you understand the climate and if that area needs some work, begin by modeling better ways to interact. Small changes are cumulative, so be consistent when implementing changes to improve the climate. When the climate improves, people respond with warmth, acceptance, invitation, and innovation. As the climate is experienced in positive ways, culture will also be crafted with shared positivity.

Award-winning author and CEO of Mindsteps, Dr. Robyn Jackson says that there is a difference between people feeling "comfortable and making people feel safe." In her May 3, 2023, podcast, she says it's a natural tendency for principals to protect teachers—protect them from extra work, from angry parents, from district office mandates, etc., and it can become a trap. Jackson says, "You can't control people's feelings, and feelings are fleeting. The more you try to make people feel comfortable, the more you become a slave to the whims of your staff." People don't like to move when they are comfortable.

When we work on making people comfortable, we put them in a position where they don't want to move. My youngest grandson loves falling asleep while I'm holding him. He will snuggle in and fall into peaceful slumber. When I move to try to lay him down in his bed, he immediately begins crying. He's comfortable and doesn't want to move even though he will sleep better in bed than he will while I'm holding him. Jackson raises this point in her podcast. When we work hard at making our staff comfortable, they don't want to move even if it will be more beneficial in the long run. As a better alternative, Jackson recommends that leaders should strive to make the staff feel safe, rather than comfortable. Jackson says:

> When people feel safe, you're not focused on their comfort. You're focused on creating conditions that make people brave enough and empowered enough to do something bigger than themselves. It allows people to do it when they're scared, when they're uncomfortable. Trying something new is uncomfortable, but if I feel safe, it means that I can try to get comfortable with my discomfort and try anyway. (Jackson 2023)

It is a relief to let go of the stress of trying to make your staff feel comfortable. That's their job. Yours is to create a culture that is safe—safe to take risks, safe to share ideas, and safe to step beyond the status quo when ideas suggest there is another way to make instruction better for students. Schools with this kind of culture, one that is grounded in shared values and beliefs, know that success is created together. Through collaboration, they examine the impact of instruction in a non-threatening, supportive environment. Authors Jenni Donohoo and Steven Katz add to this thinking and say, "When educators share the belief that they can influence student achievement, regardless of some of the difficult circumstances faced in schools today, the results can be very powerful." (2020, xiii) Safety, support, and collaboration like this create collective efficacy. A healthy school culture grows when teachers and administrators believe they can fulfill the mission, and they are committed to supporting each other while educating all students. That is what collective efficacy does.

COLLECTIVE EFFICACY IN ACTION

So, what do you think is the greatest obstacle to a healthy school culture and collective efficacy? High-stakes testing can destroy the culture and teachers' beliefs about success very quickly if left unchecked. Let me share an example.

Anna, an experienced, successful principal in Florida, was asked by her superintendent to take over as principal at a school with consistently low-performing accountability ratings. In fact, the school had been declining for ten years. The most obvious contributor to the decline was the school's low passing scores on the state assessment.

The school was in the heart of an urban area, one of the oldest neighborhoods in the city. Located just two miles down the road was a very similar school. It had the same demographics and educated the same grade levels. But there was one large difference: the other school wasn't in the low-performing range. As a result, parents at Anna's school continually asked for their children to be transferred to the neighboring school that was performing better. Usually, those transferring out were some of the higher-performing students, which hurt Anna's school even more. It was Anna's charge to uncover what was really going on behind the scenes at the low-ranking school and turn things around.

In her first few months, Anna discovered several positives about the low-ranking school. It was clean and organized. Classrooms had plenty of technology. In fact, they'd been given supplies well beyond what one might expect. The storage rooms were filled to the brim with all kinds of instructional materials: every program, manipulative, and kit imaginable. They even had technology and tools that hadn't been unboxed.

In addition, class sizes were small, teacher-student ratios low, and the expert schedule provided a period for individual teacher planning and an additional period for team collaboration. The professional learning records showed an abundant amount of training on the latest instructional strategies, programs and technology. It appeared to Anna that the district simply kept dumping more money, more supplies, and more training into the low-performing school—with less than desirable results.

In the first couple of weeks after Anna arrived, district-level personnel frequently stopped by to let her know everything that was wrong with the school. Instructional coaches, program directors, coordinators— everyone came to add their two cents. Many offered their support, but that was by throwing new training or coaching onto the already extensive pile of professional learning. Honestly, the teachers were tired of it. They couldn't get excited about teaching because they'd just had too many people trying to "fix what they were doing wrong."

So, if not the training of teachers, what then?

Anna was pleased that teachers had a planning period for lesson preparation and parent conferences as well as a period for collaboration together. She soon discovered that they were actually just using the collaboration time as an additional planning period—independently grading papers and sitting at desks spread throughout the room doing solitary work.

Anna forged a plan to better understand her new staff. She committed to spending time listening until she could fully grasp the culture of the school. Up to this point, her conversations with staff were short and superficial. Teachers and others were distrustful and fearful that the new principal would try to "fix" them too.

Anna didn't give up. She was open and transparent about not having all the answers and expressed a desire to learn from her staff. Anna asked for their opinions and listened to them. She even shared her own vulnerabilities in the process.

After months of listening, Anna decided that she didn't need to focus on the negatives. Instead, she started compiling lists of what the school was doing well. She talked about teachers' strengths and highlighted how they got things right. Over time, this built trust among the teachers and staff. Slowly, they began to trust her motives and feel heard.

This was what she had been working toward.

Anna understood that when teachers feel safe and valued, they perform better and are more likely to work together. Not only did she seek to build relationships with each staff member, but Anna also provided means for the teachers and staff to build trust among themselves.

What was typically a school with a high level of distrust slowly started becoming a school of staff and teachers who were beginning to open up to one another. This was a stark contrast to the school Anna had first encountered where teachers arrived just before the first bell and left as soon as students were dismissed each afternoon, where teachers didn't exchange ideas or talk during their collaboration time, and where teachers ate alone instead of together.

As Anna learned their stories, she heard a few common themes among them:

- There were plenty of rules and mandates.

- Compliance was expected.

- Teachers were not free to modify instruction.

- Teachers were not encouraged to take risks.

- The staff and teachers did not feel like their professional opinions mattered.

- Teachers felt as though they were not trusted by their leaders.

Once a climate of freedom had been cultivated through Anna's persistence to ask good questions, reveal her own vulnerabilities, and encourage what was going well, deeper conversations started happening. Teachers began to trust one another and discuss ways to increase learning. They felt empowered to celebrate each other's successes and identify gaps they could close—together, as part of the same team with the same goals.

As time went by, the chaotic practices of their past were streamlined and organized. They started to align with mutual goals for their current students. Teachers sorted through programs and tools, worked and planned together, and shared and supported one another like they had never done before.

Perhaps the most exciting result was that teachers started stressing less about being a low-performing school and focused more on building a community of learners—among students and teachers.

By the end of Anna's second year, the school was a different place.

Turnover that year was much lower than previous years. It wasn't all sunshine and roses, nor was it without bumps in the proverbial road. Some teachers, who had been among a toxic group resistant to change, left after Anna's first year. But they left behind a greater, in-progress work: the building of a stronger, more positive culture, one that carried into year three. After Anna's third year, their state assessment scores were the highest in the school's history. The school was finally "out of the red" and into a more progressively growing rank.

When the school culture is healthy, inclusive and supportive, students, staff and families are all more likely to be engaged. Culture impacts everything. In order to become a school where people thrive and experience consistent growth, it is important to

- Create a vision-focused continuous improvement culture

- Cultivate an environment that is safe and supportive

- Commit to a common sense of purpose, a mission

When teachers are committed to a common purpose, feel safe and heard, and welcome a culture that's continually evolving for the students' benefit, the school flourishes.

A CULTURE CHECK

Does your school's culture support continuous improvement? For an informal assessment, have your staff independently rank the statements below between 1 and 5 with one being never and five being always.

- I have a clear understanding of my school's vision, and I support its message.

- I embrace our school's mission as my own.

- Our mission inspires me to be my best.

- Our school climate is safe, healthy, and supportive.

- I am invited to participate in decision-making, and my feedback is valued.

- My voice and perspectives are valued and treated with dignity in my school.

- I feel safe sharing my ideas for new teaching strategies with others at my grade level or in my department.

- I feel safe sharing my ideas for new teaching strategies with other colleagues at my school (e.g., administrators, teachers in other departments or different grade levels).

- I am encouraged to collaborate and try new ideas with my team.

Collect the scores, add them together and divide by the number of participants. A score of 31 or above roughly indicates a school that supports continuous improvement. If you want to go deeper, score each statement individually. Of course, these questions only provide an indicator regarding continuous improvement. To truly assess the culture, consider a nationally recognized survey that provides an in-depth profile of your school. There are many empirically validated survey tools. One location to find a variety of options is on the National Center on Safe Supportive Learning Environments (NCSSLE) website at https://safesupportivelearning.ed.gov. The NCSSLE is funded through the U.S. Department of Education's Office of Safe and Supportive Schools. On this site, you will find a list of school climate surveys for grades PreK–12 and more. Additionally, you will find information about school climate measurement, data trends, and other resources.

REFLECTING ON RESISTANCE

If we know that change is driven forward by people and that data tell us what needs to be changed, why are people resistant to data dictating the road ahead of them? Because change is tough. As human beings, we naturally resist new ways of being, teaching, and making decisions. Why? Most educators are already providing everything they can to help students grow and learn. During the data analysis and research for continuous improvement, only a handful of people are typically involved. If communication is not clear and widely discussed with plenty of opportunities for clarification and repetition, the entire school may not fully understand the reasoning behind the research results or requests for change. Teachers are already doing what they feel is best for students, so why would they want to change and "experiment" with a different strategy? It is hard to hear something that is different from what you believe and then jump right up and implement big change. Teachers care. They want the very best for their students and feel like they know them in ways outside researchers may not. Consider this excerpt from Richard Sagor's *How to Conduct Collaborative Action Research* as he explains the concept of cognitive dissonance and how it relates to school improvement efforts:

> I suspect the reason schools are so slow to change is that teachers are, for the most part, already doing what they believe is best for their students. Cognitive dissonance theory tells us that to reduce stress, human beings strive for congruence between their behavior and beliefs; (Festinger 1957) therefore, teachers would have to be psychologically unbalanced to deliberately not make changes they believed would benefit their students. The fact is that many teachers have good reason to interpret colleagues' or administrators' calls for change as requests to abandon what's best for their students and instead conduct irresponsible experiments on them. You can hardly fault any teacher for resisting such requests. (Sagor 1992, 66–67)

If this is what is happening at your school, talk about it. Validate how people are feeling. Double-check the data and research together. Involve those who are having the most difficulty accepting the research results. Go back to the vision, the mission, and the core values. Recommit to doing whatever it takes to meet students' needs.

Sagor goes on to say, "What we need to realize is that the primary reason people don't change their opinion in these debates is that no evidence is offered to make them even begin to question their beliefs (i.e., their biases). And if there is no good reason to question their beliefs, which are congruent with their behavior, why go through the stress of change?" (1992, 67)

Schools where a data-driven culture thrives are those that champion the use of data. They conduct pilot programs and sometimes even establish competing pilot programs to resolve debates or to determine the best approach for their students. Remember the school in Florida where several teachers left at the end of Anna's first and second years? Teachers exited because of their unwillingness to collaboratively work together. When Anna first arrived, the culture lacked the safety, support, and encouragement teachers needed, and it took time to build. When an enthusiastic data-upholder like Anna is allowed to break through icy exteriors and is given enough time to gain support, transformation can occur. Principals are key to instigating this kind of change, but acting alone is very difficult. Principals need help as change agents. Change agents carry the torches across the length and breadth of the school. It is important to identify additional school leaders who will work collaboratively as change agents. Give them wings to fly. Support them. Invite others to listen to their ideas. Create opportunities for them to share their innovative ideas based on the findings of data collection efforts.

Two cultural beliefs that your school's change agents need to carry are that data literacy is a critical skill everyone needs to master and that the data used for the school's decision-making is trustworthy. When teachers and principals at your school regularly collect and analyze data and then make instructional decisions based on what students need, you are probably in a culture that embraces continuous improvement. When you recognize that you—and everyone around you—are crucial to the impact that data can have, you are well-equipped. In schools where team members are resourced to communicate about what test scores really mean, to identify how much impact their instruction produces, and to plan where to go next, they are driving the mission toward their vision of success.

SHIFT A SLOW-MOVING TRAIN

Collaborating is easier said than done. Asking staff to successfully pool their knowledge, ideas, and talents doesn't just happen. Training and practice are key. The classic children's book *The Little Engine That Could* is a lesson in perseverance over time. In it, a little train saves the day not through its might, but by its willingness to keep trying. Where the other larger trains were not willing to pull a long train over a steep mountain, the smaller train was eager to keep pressing on toward the goal.

As you and your team aim to influence the culture for good, keep the goal in mind. Talk about the vision and mission statements you've created. Reflect on them often. Try to incorporate them into natural conversations. Keep communicating them to teachers and staff. People need to hear them over and over before they will solidly embrace them.

In addition to communicating the school's shared vision and mission, identify and recognize and celebrate examples of the core values in action. These three, vision, mission, and core values, can make decision-making easier and actions more focused. My intermediate school created core values around the belief that students need opportunities to explore and experience multiple elective and extra-curricular offerings. This shaped our decision-making with how we elected cheerleaders, formed athletic teams, and other activities.

If your core values need to be refreshed or if you want to develop them for the first time, don't rush. Use the ideas below and create time between each one so your staff can reflect and refine their thoughts.

1. Identify common values among your team. You may start by asking team members, "What would make you proud?" Brainstorm examples of what would make the mission statement visible to onlookers in how staff and students treat one another.

2. Assign behaviors to those values. (Example: If you identify the value of exploration, the behavior you attach to that value may be, "We agree to promote teachers and students who have new ideas they'd like to try, even at the risk of looking foolish or failing.")

3. Remember that the behaviors you assign to each core value are guidelines to help everyone govern his or her own behavior and understand how to treat others. Give examples. Role-play behaviors to ensure that everyone understands.

4. Obtain a pledge from each staff member to uphold the core values. Explain that these are what you will base decisions on. They are how you will hold one another accountable and be guided back on track if you go astray. All staff needs to agree.

   a. If you have staff struggling to agree, remember that a pledge doesn't have to be 100%. Remind reluctant staff that the core values will be reviewed frequently and sometimes schools find they need to make adjustments. Ask them two questions. First, on a scale of 1 to 10, can you give it a 6?

Second, even though you don't support it 100%, can you live with it and try it for now? It's okay for the staff to be in a split agreement if your reluctantly agreeing team members feel heard and that they're not acquiescing to something they don't believe in upholding.

b. Regardless of whether or not the staff is in full agreement, select a date to review the core values. If your staff is split, pick a date no longer than 90 days out. If the staff are in agreement, the review date can be scheduled anywhere between six months to a year.

c. These tactics cannot be used to sway a team member to "your way" or to undercut someone else's differing opinion. Instead, this is one way to help a diverse-thinking staff further define what they value in their pursuit of continuous improvement. If staff feel pushed in any way, they may rebel and put up roadblocks. It is important that everyone understands it's okay to professionally share disagreements as long as you are able to talk through them and end with a mutually acceptable goal. With permission, you can say, "We have staff who are not 100% committed, but they feel they can live with it. Thank you for being willing to give it a chance. Our status check is scheduled for (date), and we will consider the implementation experiences and possibly make adjustments at that time."

BUILD-UP INSTEAD OF BUY-IN

Sometimes school leaders are afraid to move forward with change because of the lack of *buy-in*. Garnering buy-in doesn't always work. Maybe it is time for a different approach. Dr. Edie Holcomb, school improvement and reform expert, says:

The term *buy-in* implies that there's a manufactured product and that the customer must be convinced or coerced into paying for it, generating mental images of the stereotypical used car salesman pulling out all the stops to unload a lemon on some unsuspecting victim. If a mission statement or school improvement plan or district initiative has indeed been manufactured elsewhere—and that does happen sometimes—then *buy-in* is not a good use of resources. A better term than *buy-in* would be *build-up*. Engaging people *throughout* a process is a much better way to gain their commitment than expecting them to accept and support a done deal after it's been created by someone else. (Holcomb 2012, 21–22)

School leaders who engage in continuous improvement processes and have a clear understanding of the school's climate and culture do not worry about *buy-in*. When the right processes are in place and the right stakeholders are engaged, *build-up* can eliminate the need for *buy-in*.

STRESS RELIEF: A HEALTHY CULTURE

NBA coaching legend Phil Jackson, who led the Chicago Bulls and L.A. Lakers to multiple wins, said this about culture: "The strength of the team is each member. The strength of each member is the team." (Goodreads, n.d.)

Building a healthy culture takes time and concerted effort. Below are more ideas to help you identify and strengthen your school's culture.

1. **Conduct an activity that looks toward the future.** Remind staff that climate is how people feel and culture is about how they act. Ask staff to dream of the perfect climate and culture as they write their answers to these questions. Then, discuss them.

   • What do we want students to be doing and how do we want them to feel in classrooms three years from now?

   • How will teachers be working and feeling three years from now?

   • What will you hear about our school in the community three years from now?

   • How will our stakeholders feel about our school? How will they be engaged?

   • Do our mission and vision, as evidenced in our core values, move us toward accomplishing these three-year desires? Why or why not?

- How does our current culture align with the questions above? What do we need to do to make the above become reality?

2. **Encourage staff to take a larger role in leading the school.** For example, have teachers examine their own strengths and needs. Have them be in charge of their own professional learning by creating a professional learning plan for the year.

3. **Organize internal field trips.** Visit each other's classrooms or professional learning communities/collaboration meetings. Encourage the sharing of ideas and processes among disciplines. Celebrate supporting each other. Encourage risk-taking and experimenting to strengthen alignment between grade levels and content areas.

4. **Strengthen awareness.** Finally, be encouraged by the work you are doing and never stop gathering information about the school's culture. Changing a school's culture can be a huge challenge and will not happen overnight. But, recognizing the power of culture and how it defines "the way we do things" is an important step for school leaders. Seek input from people who are new. What do they see and feel? The culture is much easier for them to see than those who have been at the school for several years.

In 2002, the journal *Educational Leadership* published an article by Roland S. Barth, founding director of the Principals' Center at Harvard University. In this article we read:

> When we come to believe that our schools should be providing a school culture that creates and sustains a community of student and adult learning—that this is the trellis of our profession—then we will organize our schools, classrooms, and learning experiences differently. Show me a school where instructional leaders constantly examine the school's culture and work to transform it into one hospitable to sustained human learning, and I'll show you students who do just fine on those standardized tests. (Barth 2002, 11)

It is easy to want to jump right into data analysis when beginning a continuous improvement planning cycle. However, without a supportive culture that embraces continuous improvement, you might find yourself floundering in a sea of data with no productive results. Continuous improvement will never become an effective core operating system without a healthy culture to support it. The good news is that culture and continuous improvement can successfully grow together. Continue working on culture while you—together—tackle the next step: identifying the most important data for continuous improvement.

Chapter 4

DATA - GETTING ORGANIZED

> *"Data are just summaries of thousands of stories—tell a few of those stories to help make data meaningful." Chip & Dan Heath*

What do a glass of orange juice and a school's accountability rating have in common? Both have an origin story full of connecting parts that are linked together like a chain. The links are important because the chain is only strong when *all* the links are solidly connected. If any of the links snap, the chain cannot do its work and a story of success cannot be told.

The ability to enjoy orange juice for breakfast depends on a connected supply chain process to get from the orange groves to the kitchen table. This story involves farmers, fruit pickers, machinery, factory workers, packaging, delivery drivers, grocery stockers, and you—shopping at the store. During the 2020 pandemic, many people who had never considered how the supply chain impacts their grocery list started seeing empty grocery store shelves. The supply chain that had previously been taken for granted suddenly became very important to consumers.

A school's success documented in an accountability rating has a supply chain story, too. The context and environment of learning influences a multitude of processes and procedures by which the school makes decisions around curriculum, instruction, and assessment. Culture, teacher quality, and experience also are linked with school performance. It's a complicated story and each school is unique. Making judgments about a school after only looking at the accountability rating is the same as judging the quality of the grocery store by the empty shelves during the height of the 2020 pandemic. We can't know the store's story or the school's with just one look and just one perspective. We may miss important details. Every school has its own story to tell through a rich variety of data. The needs assessment is the place to record it.

ANALYZING SCHOOL DATA

The topic of analyzing data for a needs assessment isn't a popular one among some educators. One problem is that often those educators see data analysis for the whole school as separate and different from the work they regularly do with data. The truth is, it *IS* different. Most educators regularly work with data in their area(s) of responsibility– but they don't work with *all* of the data in the school. The good news is that the data analysis process for the entire school doesn't have to be complicated. It doesn't have to be done start-to-finish in one long, formal meeting. In fact, doing so may be one of the most ineffective ways to analyze the school's data. When creating something as important as the data analysis that will be used to construct a plan for the school's growth, it is important to take the time needed to do things right.

So how do you begin? Schools collect enormous volumes of data, but most educators are only aware of small parts of this data set—usually the data that are closest to their job assignment. The result is that they have a narrow and fragmented understanding of the school. That is no fault of the educator; it is due to the structure of school operations. Without effective procedures where educators can share and interpret data with one another, schools fall back to only reporting what is easiest to report— the school's ratings on the latest state assessment. One way to prevent that is to establish different teams to build the comprehensive needs assessment (CNA). The initial phase is data analysis. This is considered a snapshot because it includes the latest data available. But the work of data analysis is never completed. All new data is analyzed as it becomes available and the cycle continues. So, who does the analysis and data interpretation?

CONTINUOUS IMPROVEMENT NEEDS ASSESSMENT AND PLANNING TEAMS

To simplify what can become a cumbersome process, establish two teams as standing committees to develop the CNA snapshot and keep the CNA current. Sometimes you may also need to temporarily add additional ad hoc teams. The data teams are described below:

1. **Data Organization Team (DOT):** This is a core team of about 4-6 people who are responsible for gathering, organizing, and interpreting data and keeping the CNA current. The team meets monthly checking for data needs, analyzing new data, and reporting information to the Advisory Committee. The DOT doesn't have to be a new committee. There may already be a team who can take on these duties. Select people who believe in examining the impact instruction has on student learning and using that information to change adult practices. The DOT must be knowledgeable about the school's programs and processes. Additional characteristics for the DOT include:

   • Representative group—representing different roles among the staff such as administrators, data coaches, assessment coordinators, teachers, and support staff and representative of the school community's racial and ethnic diversity.

   • Committed to continuous improvement—exhibiting a growth mindset

   • Strong organization and communication skills

   • Dependable, non-judgmental, and confidential

   • At least one member needs to have full access to all data portals used by the school

   • At least one team member should be proficient with spreadsheets or other data organization structures

2. **Advisory Committee:** This is a larger team of stakeholders representing groups such as teachers and other school staff, families and community members, administrators, and students (middle

and high schools). Try to keep this team under 20 members and be sure the membership is representative of the demographics of the students. The Advisory Committee provides input and feedback on the data analysis and other needs assessment components. Later, they also provide input on the goals, performance objectives, and strategies in the continuous improvement plan. The committee meets 4-6 times per year (or as needed) with the DOT. Some state and federal programs have requirements for certain stakeholders to be members of this committee. There may also be membership election requirements, so be sure to check your district and state policies.

3. **Temporary Ad Hoc Planning Teams:** These are smaller, temporary groups of 2-5 stakeholders knowledgeable about certain topic areas in the continuous improvement plan. They convene when needed. Often that is later in the process - when it is time to create strategies. However, the DOT may want an Ad Hoc Planning Team to review their data analysis before the information is presented to the Advisory Committee. These teams are temporary and people are typically assigned to these roles.

WHAT DO THE TEAMS DO?

To assist with the development of the CNA snapshot, the DOT first looks at the data. The data gathering process begins with spreadsheets, copies of assessment results, survey results, anecdotal records, etc. It can get complicated, and the DOT's first focus is to reduce confusion for the Advisory Committee by organizing the data in meaningful ways. One of the best ways to do this is through a *narrative interpretation* of the data. Busy stakeholders trying to develop a CNA typically do not have the time or the background to fully interpret numbers on a chart. So, charts and graphs are always accompanied by a narrative. One key action for the CNA process is to identify the *why* behind the data results, including identifying the root causes of problems. Providing a narrative helps build an understanding of what is preventing higher levels of student learning. Each data source has its own unique reporting format making it difficult to compare information. It is the DOT's responsibility to show links and connections between all data so that the Advisory Committee can understand and consider the results. The results are then measured against the grade level standards to reveal strengths and problems. The Advisory Committee will help provide direction to prioritize and develop strategies for the strengths and problems.

WHAT DATA DO WE HAVE?

Schools are drowning in data and helping to make sense of what is most meaningful is the DOT's first responsibility. Teachers, attendance clerks, principals, counselors—many roles already use data on a regular basis and that is good news. The DOT doesn't have to start from scratch. Often the needed data are already being gathered, analyzed, and used as part of someone's regular responsibilities. Start by taking inventory of what data resources currently exist and who uses them. Set aside a few minutes during a faculty meeting to brainstorm all the data available – even individual classroom data could be valuable for the CNA. List your school's data inventory in a chart like the one in Figure 4.1 below. Not all the data will be used in your CNA, but knowing what *is* available can be a time-saving asset as you make plans to gather data.

Figure 4.1 School Data Inventory

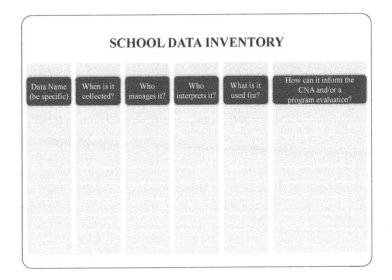

SCHOOL DATA INVENTORY

Data Name (be specific)	When is it collected?	Who manages it?	Who interprets it?	What is it used for?	How can it inform the CNA and/or a program evaluation?

In addition to the information gained through the School Data Inventory, another question to ask is about other similar work that might have been completed as part of a program application or program evaluation. If data has been recently analyzed for other reasons, use it. Don't replicate data analysis if the past analysis is still relevant. Also, acknowledge the potential and limitations of some of the data. Due to collection method, date, sample size, and other factors some data may be less valid and reliable than other data. Recognize the shortcomings, but do not simply disregard certain sets of data due to perceptions of quality.

WHAT DATA DO WE NEED?

Schools may need to collect various types of data to conduct a needs assessment depending on the purpose of the assessment. If you are creating the needs assessment in response to a specific program or as part of an accountability requirement, look to the program for guidance on needs assessment requirements. If your needs assessment will satisfy more than one program, it is helpful to begin by listing the program goals to determine what data options can be used to measure the school's success towards meeting the goals.

Many programs' priorities overlap, making it easy to use data for more than one purpose. An example is shown below in Figure 4.2. Let's say that our needs assessment is for Head Start, Title I and Title II. We list all three programs and reflect on the program goals. What data might we use to measure our school's progress toward reaching the program goals? After we brainstorm data options, we can then look down the column to see if the same data is used for more than one program. We can see that our local benchmark assessments and the state assessment measure progress for both Title I program goals and Title II program goals. We can analyze the data from those assessments once and produce information that is relevant to both federal programs. This helps us be more efficient and thorough with the information produced during the data analysis.

Figure 4.2 Data Options to Measure Program Goals

Needs Assessment Data to Measure Program Goals

	What are the program's goals?	What data can we use to measure progress toward achieving the program's goals?
Head Start	• Provide developmental, academic, economic, and social opportunities for school readiness for young children from low-income families.	• Family surveys • ELOF observation-based assessments
Title I	• Provide all children significant opportunity to receive a fair, equitable, and high-quality education, and to close educational achievement gaps.	• Local benchmark assessment • State assessment data
Title II	• Students' mastery of standards. • Quality and effectiveness of teachers, principals, and other school leaders.	• Local benchmark assessment • Staff surveys • State assessment data

After identifying data to measure progress on the program goals, be sure to also look into the program requirements. Some federal programs have specific requirements for certain types of data and the student groups to assess.

Most schools want to complete a CNA snapshot to meet the requirements of all federal and state programs and to inform their continuous improvement work. Figure 4.3 includes common data that schools, including Title I schools, may need to collect for a needs assessment.

Figure 4.3 Data Commonly Used in a CNA

Examples of Data Sources*

Student Demographic Data

- Race/ethnicity
- Gender
- Poverty level
- Languages spoken

- Rate and type of disabilities
- Homelessness status

- Migrant status
- Foster care status
- Mobility rates

Student Academic Data

- State assessments
- District, grade level, or subject area assessments
- Career & Technology participation and grades

- Grades
- Graduation rates
- College/career readiness
- Special education achievement
- Section 504 achievement

- Gifted/talented achievement
- Extra-curricular participation

Student Behavior Data

- Wellness indicators
- Attendance rates

- Dropout rates
- Discipline rates

- Safety information
- Perceptions of school

Staff Data

- Professional staff qualifications, certifications, and experience
- Attendance rates

- Paraprofessionals' qualifications, certifications, and experience
- Race/ethnicity/languages
- Perceptions of school

- Recruitment/retention information
- Professional learning needs/requests/skills

Family/Community Data

- School engagement
- Income levels
- Employment rates and opportunities

- Growth
- Crime rates
- Perceptions of school

- Other survey data
- Mobility rates
- Migrant staus

*Not an all-inclusive list.

ORGANIZING THE DATA

Data can be organized in a variety of ways for the needs assessment process. Most schools opt for a framework that groups the data around a concept. Several states have frameworks based on the research of effective practices. Two examples are the Texas Effective Schools Framework and The New York City Department of Education's Framework for Great Schools. These frameworks add clarity as schools seek to develop strategies to optimize student achievement. Most frameworks also include guidance with data analysis, finding root causes, and developing focused plans. Each framework organizes data a little differently, but there are often common threads. You can see similarities with the two example frameworks in Figure 4.4 below.

Figure 4.4 Two Example Frameworks

Similarities Between Frameworks

Texas Effective Schools Framework	New York Framework for Great Schools
Strong School Leadership and Planning	Effective School Leadership
Strategic Staffing	Collaborative Teachers
Positive School Culture	Supportive Environment
Effective Instruction	Rigorous Instruction
N/A	Trust
High-Quality Instructional Materials & Assessments	N/A

If your school or district doesn't have a framework, an Internet search will reveal a variety of valid and researched frameworks for continuous improvement. Opt for simplicity and clarity in the framework you select. The best frameworks have between 4-6 elements. Within your selected framework, the needs assessment process looks to identify the strengths or what is going well and the needs or problems that need to be addressed.

WHERE TO START

Begin your needs assessment work by creating a chart with the school's demographics data and the latest state assessment data. Regardless of whether you are conducting a full comprehensive needs assessment or a smaller needs assessment for just one program, these are the two pieces of data to analyze first. They are the starting points for conversations about the school's strengths and problems. The DOT can compile this information ahead of time so that when the full Continuous Improvement Advisory Committee meets, they can reflect on key findings to jumpstart the focus for further conversations. Sometimes this data is available from the state on a dashboard or in reports received from the testing company. If using those, be sure that there's not so much extra information on the form that it is hard to find and see this basic information. See Figure 4.5 below for an example of how to list the demographics and state assessment scores.

The DOT can complete all but two columns. The "Possible Implications for our School" column and the "Possible Implications for Instruction" column should be completed by the Advisory Committee after some discussion. For an extra level of information, in addition to discussing the strengths and problems, look at this data from the "challenges" perspective. A challenge is not the same as a problem. For example, if the attendance boundaries are redrawn and the percent of students on free or reduced lunch increases by 25%, that could be a challenge for some teachers. We would never identify that as a problem, but it might be a challenge—especially at the beginning. Teachers will need to adjust instruction and use strategies for acceleration and enrichment for students who need that extra boost. Challenges are important to recognize, even if they never make it into the plan.

Figure 4.5: State Assessment Data by Student Groups

STATE ASSESSMENT DATA BY STUDENT GROUPS								
Student Groups	Number in group	% Of Students	3-Year Changes/ Trends	Possible Implications for our School	Passing Rates	Advanced Level Rates	3-Year Changes/ Trends	Possible Implications for Instruction
Race/ Ethnicity (list each student group on a separate line)								
Poverty Level								
English Learners/ Emergent Bilinguals								
Students with Disabilities								
Migrant								
Homeless								
Neglected/ Delinquent								
Foster Care								
Military Connected								
Gifted/Talented								
College/Career-Ready								

Remember that this data is a *starting point* for the needs assessment process. This does not tell your school's story nor is it enough to develop your continuous improvement plan (CIP).

STRESS RELIEF: EXAMINE OUR DATA PRACTICES

As you and your team consider getting organized with data before the analysis processes, it may be helpful to examine your history and perception of needs assessments. Answer the following questions as a group. They will help identify what may need to be done prior to the data analysis:

1. Have we completed the School Data Inventory located in this chapter?

2. Do we have data collection practices that are not reflected on the School Data Inventory? If so, what are they?

3. Do we have a list of the programs at our school that require a needs assessment?
    a. If so, what are they and when are they due? Can they all be conducted at the same time?
    b. If not, assign a team to create one and determine the deadline.

4. Who can serve as our DOT to analyze, interpret, and summarize our data?

5. Where will the DOT document their work? How will it be reported to the Advisory Committee?

6. How can we be sure that the right stakeholders have opportunities to review and provide feedback on the data? How do we determine which stakeholders need to attend what meetings?

7. How do we ensure simplicity without sacrificing meaning? How can we simplify the process?

Chapter 5

DATA - FINDING MEANING

> *"Not everything that can be counted counts and not everything that counts can be counted." Albert Einstein*

What pops into your mind when you hear the word data? For many people, it's numbers. To understand the numbers in schools, it is imperative that we consider data from a variety of sources. Teaching and learning are complicated. One of the best ways to gain an understanding of results is to think about them from different angles or perspectives.

Dr. Victoria L. Bernhardt, Executive Director of the Education for the Future Initiative, focuses her work on how learning organizations gather, analyze, and use data. Her structure for comprehensive data analysis, titled Multiple Measures of Data, guides the use of all data so that the school's focus is not solely on improving individual students who are not achieving on measures used for compliance. She says, "Knowing where a school is now is the part of planning for continuous school improvement that requires a comprehensive and honest look at all the school's data—not just student learning results." (Bernhardt 2013, 15) She goes on to say that a comprehensive look at where the school is now helps schools understand *how* they are getting their results—what is working and what isn't. "Schools committed to using comprehensive data analysis to continuously improve their learning organization are able to blend creativity with discipline to create their future. Schools focused only on gaps and compliance can neither innovate nor create a future that looks different from the status quo." (2013, 3) Bernhardt's structure involves gathering the data needed to answer the following four questions:

1. Who are we?

2. How do we do business?

3. How are our students doing?

4. What are our processes?

The data collected to answer the questions above naturally falls into four categories that make up Dr. Bernhardt's Multiple Measures of Data. See the Venn Diagram shown in Figure 5.1.

Figure 5.1: Multiple Measures (Bernhardt 2013)

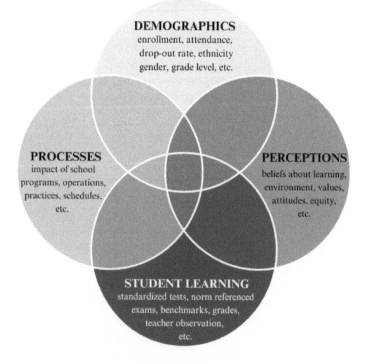

This graphic illustrates how student achievement data provide only one perspective. There are three other perspectives that are beneficial to consider. Each of the four have overlapping areas where data can be considered through more than one perspective. The four Multiple Measures perspectives are:

- **Demographics** to understand students, staff, and community.

- **Student learning** to understand what students know and do not know, with respect to what we want them to know.

- **Perceptions** to understand what students want to do in the future and how they prefer to learn, plus gauging staff and parent perceptions of the learning environment.

- **School processes** to understand what processes have been implemented to obtain the results the school has been getting over time. (Bernhardt, 2018)

Looking at data through each of Bernhardt's four categories creates a perspective to provide deep understanding with a wide range of meaningful information. For example, if a school team is asked to disaggregate data on English Learners/Emergent Bilinguals and they are not looking at different types of data and thinking from multiple perspectives, they might ask some very basic questions:

- How many students are English Learners/Emergent Bilinguals?

- What are their races, ethnicities, and grade levels?

- How are they doing academically?

The team might stop after asking those three questions. However, if the school team is prompted to build their questions through the four Multiple Measures categories, they will usually ask deeper questions and gain a more meaningful understanding of the successes and challenges for English Learners/Emergent Bilinguals. Examples of questions using the Multiple Measures categories are listed in Figure 5.2 below.

Figure 5.2 Multiple Measures Questions

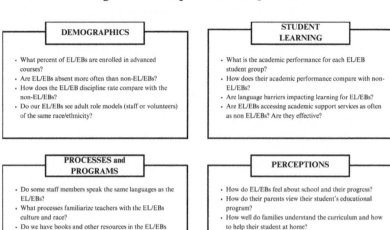

DEMOGRAPHICS

- What percent of EL/EBs are enrolled in advanced courses?
- Are EL/EBs absent more often than non-EL/EBs?
- How does the EL/EB discipline rate compare with the non-EL/EBs?
- Do our EL/EBs see adult role models (staff or volunteers) of the same race/ethnicity?

STUDENT LEARNING

- What is the academic performance for each EL/EB student group?
- How does their academic performance compare with non-EL/EBs?
- Are language barriers impacting learning for EL/EBs?
- Are EL/EBs accessing academic support services as often as non EL/EBs? Are they effective?

PROCESSES and PROGRAMS

- Do some staff members speak the same languages as the EL/EBs?
- What processes familiarize teachers with the EL/EBs culture and race?
- Do we have books and other resources in the EL/EBs languages or that support/celebrate their cultures and ethnicities?
- In what ways are EL/EBs involved/engaged with school activities?

PERCEPTIONS

- How do EL/EBs feel about school and their progress?
- How do their parents view their student's educational program?
- How well do families understand the curriculum and how to help their student at home?

An important thing to note with the four categories is that we can only make direct changes in one area—in processes and programs. The best we can do in the other areas is to provide influence. For example, the first category is demographics. We don't have any say about which families move into the attendance area and send their children to our school. We welcome and embrace them all, but we can't change the demographics category. The next category is student learning. Hopefully, we have a strong influence in the student learning category, but at the end of the day, the students are the ones who must learn.

Next are perceptions. We have influence with perceptions, but we can't command people to believe something or feel a certain way. Processes and programs are different. We *can* determine what our master schedule looks like, when we offer tutorials, etc. So, the processes and programs category is the only category we can directly change. That doesn't mean we only focus on that one category. Not at all. What it means is that we must deeply understand demographics, perceptions and student learning.

Dr. Bernhardt says that analyzing data in each of the four Multiple Measures categories is "crucial for knowing where a learning organization is right now, and for cleaning up the system so that the organization can operate with greatest efficiency." (Bernhardt 2013, l02) Beyond that, the next step for a school is to figure out what can be done differently to get better results. "To understand how the organization is getting the results it is getting now, what is working/what is not working, and to learn more about what to do differently to get different results, we need to go deeper into the data to get answers to these and other significant questions." (2013, 102)

Going deeper into the data means looking across more than one of the Multiple Measures categories at the same time. In other words, what can we learn if we look at Student Learning by School Processes or Student Learning by School Processes by Perceptions? Analyzing a cross section of data can lead to a deeper, more valuable understanding of the meaning of the data. Figure 5.3 below explains what the data can tell us and gives an example.

Figure 5.3 Bernhardt's Multiple Measures Intersections

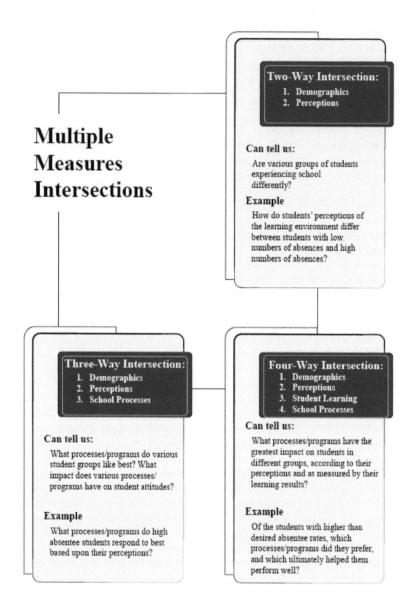

(Bernhardt 2013, 103)

For more examples, see the detailed view of Bernhardt's Venn Diagram located in Appendix A. The diagram contains example questions describing the depth of information that can be learned when you use more than one of the Multiple Measures of Data categories at the same time.

THE BIG PICTURE - THEMES IN DATA

Once your continuous improvement Advisory Committee has gone deep with data analysis using the Multiple Measures in your needs assessment framework, take a step back and look at what has been discovered. What is the big picture? Are there common themes running through the needs assessment data? You can use this list of guiding questions to help you:

- What do strengths or successful student outcomes look like? How do you know? How is the evidence displayed?

- Where are the greatest academic problems or learning gaps? What data points confirm the problems or learning gaps?

- Are there other problems (attendance, discipline, etc.) that could be contributing to the academic problems?

Make lists of the strengths and problems. School teams often focus solely on the problems, but that is a mistake. Identify and celebrate the strengths! Look carefully at them to see what can be learned from their success. It is important to list the strengths in the CNA so that later in the process, when strategies are being developed, nothing gets in the way of the strengths being continued. Sometimes strategies can even be added to areas of strength for a quick win. Keep the strengths out front so they are recognized and protected.

In Chapter 6 we will explore how to find the root causes of the problems but for now, we simply want to identify them.

STATE ASSESSMENT DATA:
WHAT STORY DOES IT TELL?

We can't expect the data from the state assessment to fulfill all requirements for a comprehensive needs assessment. Those scores are not enough. Anthony Bryk, President Emeritus of the Carnegie Foundation for the Advancement of Teaching, and colleagues' researched state assessments and how the results can be used in schools. They found that state assessments must be designed so they can be administered broadly across all kinds of schools. Some schools are large and located in urban areas. Some are small and rural. The design must work for all students, regardless of where they live, their background experiences, race, ethnicity, etc. Additionally, the assessments must be given at multiple grade levels and in multiple subject areas. "However, this generic quality also exacts a price: while the measures can signal where improvements are needed, they rarely provide the detail needed to help teachers and schools actually improve." (Bryk et al. 2015, 91)

State assessments tell schools what needs to improve, but not how. It makes no sense, then, to solely use the state assessment data as a needs assessment. State assessment data, including longitudinal data, are an important part of the comprehensive needs assessment process, but alone, the data do not tell the whole story. The state assessment data must be used in conjunction with other data and include multiple perspectives.

Another reason why the state assessment data shouldn't be used alone is that viewing it is looking back at the past. It answers, "How well did we do?" There is value in asking that question and studying the results. However, every year, conditions vary because students are different. Answering the question gives us perspective and a starting place especially if we look at the longitudinal data.

Benchmark assessments, classroom quizzes, and other current data are looking at now. They answer, "Are we on track for doing well on the summative exam?" These data allow us to alter our actions if we do not like the progress we are currently making. Last year's state assessment data and this year's benchmark assessment data are both needed for continuous improvement.

CNA DATA ANALYSIS PROTOCOL

As you seek to find evidence of the school's current status, use the questions that arise to determine what areas to explore more deeply. Exploring data in depth with a group of stakeholders who have skills ranging from, "I've never analyzed school data" all the way to, "I analyze school data all the time" can be a challenge—especially when you want to hear perspectives from all participants. The CNA Data Analysis Protocol found in Appendix B can help. One of the easiest protocols to understand and implement, the Data Analysis Protocol takes about an hour to conduct. Part of the power of this tool is that every person's voice counts. You begin with a facilitator providing an overview of the data that everyone has in front of them. The facilitator explains what the data is, where it comes from, and how it is used. The facilitator is very careful to speak in plain language without using acronyms that stakeholders might not understand. The stakeholders are given a few moments of quiet to just observe the data. The protocol begins with a round-robin opportunity for people to simply state what they notice, like this:

- I noticed this data is for two years—last year and the year before.

- I noticed there were over a hundred more students last year than there were the year before.

- I noticed the scores in the "All Students" group went up in grades 3 and 5, but stayed nearly the same in grade 4.

- I noticed that the English Learners/Emergent Bilinguals scored at least 15 points lower than their peers at every grade level.

Each "I noticed" statement is recorded. There are no right or wrong answers, and the team keeps going around the circle, giving everyone an opportunity to tell what they noticed. The next step is to give the group time to quietly think about all of the "I noticed" statements. Then, in a round-robin order, each participant makes an "I wonder how…" or "I wonder why…" or "I wonder whether…" statement. The "I wonder" statements are recorded next to the linked "I noticed" statements. (See an example format in Appendix B.) Again, the group is given a time of quiet to think—this time, about the "I wonder" statements.

The next step is to mark through anything that the school cannot control. With the remaining statements, look for trends, similar statements, and patterns. Do some statements rise to being more significant than others? Are there statements that many people responded to? Can we see emerging strengths and problems? Do we need additional data and more time to consider the "I wonder…" statements? You can find additional steps to take in Appendix B.

This process makes it "safe" to brainstorm together and prevents one or two people from dominating the conversation. Using the CNA Data Analysis Protocol will help you determine true problems so that you won't build a plan based upon hunches, assumptions, or trivia.

THE TAIL WAGGING THE DOG

Teachers evaluate data every day and may feel that they don't need a protocol to analyze school-wide data. Here is a cautionary tale of what can happen without a protocol in place:

A team of kindergarten to 3rd grade teachers was charged to write strategies for reading instruction in their school's continuous improvement plan. They met to review their school's data. A quick study of last year's school's assessment data revealed that 72% of 3rd grade students were reading below grade level. This percentage was up from 65% the year before and 62% the year before that. The group's attention quickly turned to brainstorming ideas about how the after-school tutorial program could be expanded. This tale reveals several data analysis problems that are commonly found in schools.

First, data analysis only using the 3rd grade state assessment data won't provide the complete story of how students are doing in kindergarten through 3rd grade. State assessment data is from the previous year and doesn't fully represent the students currently in those grades. Second, the state assessment data typically doesn't go deep enough to reveal the exact problem areas, and the group didn't attempt to find a root cause.

Third, it is too soon to explore a solution (how to expand the current tutorials). There isn't enough information to determine the complete problem with a root cause or causes. Educators are always solution oriented. It is common to skip over defining the complete problem to begin searching for the solution. When a problem exists, we want to "fix it" and do it quickly. But closing the learning gaps requires time. Time to dig deeply into the data. Time to think about the problem, and explore root causes before creating solution strategies. Jumping too soon to a solution is like the tail wagging the dog, and it can have unintended long-term consequences.

The school's instructional program is complicated. There are many programs and practices in place. When schools don't fully understand the problem, they sometimes opt for an "add-on" solution (expand the current tutorials) instead of exploring more effective approaches, such as strengthening Tier 1 instruction. Strengthening Tier 1 instruction may be more time-consuming to design and implement, but in the long-run, strong Tier 1 instruction is always going to have a greater impact on student success than any supplemental program. This is especially true when the design and implementation are based upon a thorough analysis of the data.

FREQUENT DATA REVIEW

In their book *Data-Driven Leadership,* Amanda Datnow and Vicki Park state that one key to building a culture of continuous improvement is by encouraging frequent reflection on a wide array of data on an ongoing basis at all levels of the system. They go on to explain that making decisions based on data is not a straight line that starts with point A and goes directly to point B. This is where the DOT can help. The data organization team meets monthly throughout the year to organize and review new data as it becomes available. They keep the school's data up-to-date and available for the continuous improvement status checks and any other group needing support through data.

This data support is extremely beneficial for busy educators who don't often have the luxury of extended time to make decisions. The DOT's work can lead school leaders and others toward being inquiry and analysis focused with their use of data. Although the DOT gathers, organizes, and does some of the initial data analysis, they don't do *all* of the analysis for the school. It is critical that all school leaders and teachers know how to analyze and interpret student data. The DOT's work also helps them look at the big picture—at a systems level view instead of solely a grade level view.

A key component of data-informed leadership is moving toward more complex definitions of what counts as student learning and of what informs how we think about student learning. Documenting the level of student engagement in the classroom through observations can be more enlightening and lead to greater innovations in teaching and learning than simply examining test scores on a page. (Datnow and Park 2014, 118–119)

Continuing the story of the Kindergarten - 3rd grade teachers charged with improving reading instruction, the teachers learned to use the CNA Data Analysis Protocol. (See Appendix B.) They used the protocol in each grade level on their local benchmark data. When they met together to compare findings, they were surprised to find several common areas in their grade level standards where students were not doing well. For example, in all four grades, students scored poorly at making inferences and using evidence to support understanding. That was eye-opening for the teachers, and they realized that strengthening Tier 1 instruction was more important than making changes to their tutorials. By continuing this process through the rest of the year and reviewing new data on a regular basis, the K-3rd teachers were able to identify and fill in the instructional gaps. The result was that in only three short years, the 3rd grade state assessment scores rose 44 points! The willingness of teachers to regularly study the impact of their instruction on student learning made this happen.

"Systems thinking is the process of understanding how things influence one another within a whole. In learning organizations, systems consist of people, structures, programs, and processes that work together to help organizations get the results they want. Continuous improvement processes work hand in glove with systems thinking to ensure healthy learning organizations." (Bernhardt 2017, p. 5)

FRAMING DATA INTO A NARRATIVE

Once the continuous improvement Advisory Committee understands the current data and the analysis is completed, it's time to weave the information together into a beautiful multicolored blanket, a needs assessment summary story. State assessment results don't reveal the entire plot. They may show the climax or the turning point of the rising action, but they do not illustrate an entire story arc. They're just facts– and facts aren't as memorable as stories.

"Stories engage our senses, and our brains respond by making sense of information more completely. They create a powerful connection and bring us closer together. Stories have the magical ability to fully immerse listeners and elicit a sense of empathy, urgency, or even great affliction. They move us to act." (Duarte 2019, pp. 3–6)

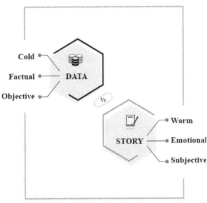

The narrative is a summary that is shaped by what you know. Not everyone can speak the language of data, so you need to make data speak the language of your stakeholders. Putting data in context is the key to making it accessible. A separate summary can be written for each area in the needs assessment framework or you can combine everything into one summary. Tell about the data analysis process and what you found. Discuss the types of data and the overall reflections. Discuss major findings and explain anything needing clarification. Explain where the data are stored so that it can be available, if needed. Below the narrative, include a list of the identified strengths and the identified problems. We are not yet ready for strategies or solutions. We are simply looking for a summary.

- What data did we examine?

- How does the data confirm what we already know?

- What have we learned?

- What does the data tell us about our school's progress?

- What questions continue to be unanswered?

- Who contributed to the summary and from what perspective (students, teachers, families, community, administrators, or other roles)?

This becomes the initial arc of your story. When you combine this with your goals, performance objectives and strategies (GPS), these data become the baseline to measure our next steps of growth. This is our beginning of the year snapshot.

STRESS RELIEF: MULTIPLE MEASURES OF DATA

A good way to simplify your data finding is to group the data by the four Multiple Measures categories. Regardless of the CNA framework your district or state chooses to use, the school's data will always align in these four areas. Grouping data according to the Multiple Measures categories can help you be sure that you are not focusing too heavily on one area, such as student learning. All four categories are important. To be able to prioritize the greatest problems and identify root causes, you need to be sure you have the complete story - the most important information. They will help you identify what your school may need to overcome to understand the meaning of data.

As with Alice in the classic Lewis Carroll tale *Alice in Wonderland*, you may be at a point where simply finding problems does not seem to help. Hang on, and don't get discouraged. Unlike Alice, who doesn't actually learn anything while she is in Wonderland, this process will help you learn how to serve students well on a continual basis. The next chapter will help you clarify needs, develop them into problem statements, and find the root cause or causes.

Chapter 6

PROBLEMS AND ROOT CAUSES

> *"It's so much easier to suggest solutions when*
> *you don't know too much about the problem."*
> *Malcolm Forbes*

You've analyzed your current data and determined strengths and needs, but what now? Before the goals, performance objectives and strategies (GPS) can be developed, it is important to transform needs into problem statements and identify the root causes or why the problems exist. When schools work on the same problems year after year with little or no progress, the issue might be a misalignment between the problem and the strategies. This is where finding the root causes makes an important difference.

PROBLEM VS. NEED

What is a problem? In continuous improvement planning, it is important to clearly define the problem you want to solve before spending time and resources generating solutions. Defining a problem is different from defining a need. So, what is the difference and why make this a big deal? A problem statement describes an unfavorable condition found in the school's data that prevents a performance objective from being achieved. It sounds like the same thing as a need, right? You might be thinking,

"Why make things more complicated?" Even the Every Student Succeeds Act (ESSA) uses the term "need." Throughout this book, I've stressed keeping things simple to reduce the stress of planning. Simplicity should always be our choice, except that in this instance I believe it is more beneficial to use the term "problem." Here's why. The term "need" is generally used in seeking funding for programs or services. It points toward a solution and stops people from considering other options. Look at these two statements. They represent the same issue:

- Written as a need: Our school needs another math teacher.

- Written as a problem: 32% of 8th graders taking eighth grade math failed while only 8% of these same students failed math as 7th graders.

Which of those two statements brings more questions to your mind? It's the version written as a problem, right? When an issue is written as a need, it is easy to be more generic and rarely generates a lively conversation. From the needs perspective, you might ask, "Why?" and receive an answer like this: "The eighth grade classes are larger than the seventh grade classes." That seems to satisfy the need and no more probing is needed. The conversation ends. We found a solution.

Alternatively, a problem statement—in the name alone—implies that you plan to provide a solution. Problem statements are typically more detailed, and the details create curiosity. Thinking from a problem statement perspective might produce a conversation like this: "There is a big difference between an 8% failure rate and a 32% failure rate. What is happening? Also, you said the 8th graders who take eighth grade math are failing. Is there another option for math?" Response: "Eighth grade math classes are larger because we also offer Algebra 1. The top students go into Algebra 1. Additionally, two eighth grade teachers also teach a period of athletics. Because they are coaches, they are not able to offer tutorials before or after school. And, on out-of-town game days, their last period math classes have substitutes because the coaches must leave early." Simply put, problem statements usually produce more questions and deeper thinking. Stating it as a need makes it sound like a cut-and-dried issue that doesn't require any more conversation. Stating the issue as a problem invites strategic thinking and more conversation, which creates a better opportunity to discover the real root causes. Simply adding another teacher will not solve all the problems in this scenario. To devise the best solution to problems, we must first identify their cause, so let's do everything possible to promote strategic, problem-solving thinking.

People don't always know what they need. That is especially true when what they need is new and unfamiliar. Henry Ford changed the world when he established the Ford Motor Company and rolled out the Model T cars. A famous quote, attributed to Ford says, "If I asked people what they wanted, they would have said faster horses." In continuous improvement, it is our responsibility to discover and understand real needs. One way to help people look beyond the obvious is to write problem statements instead of needs.

WHAT GOES IN A PROBLEM STATEMENT?

A problem statement is concise, and it identifies a specific problem that can be verified by facts. It also includes specific details (who, what, when, and where). The details are important because problem statements directly influence at least one performance objective. (More on that in Ch. 7.) Problem statements describe the unfavorable conditions that prevent the performance objective, and ultimately the goal, from being achieved. Here are the characteristics to keep in mind as you develop problem statements. Quality problem statements:

- Clearly define the problem that arises out of the data analyses.

- Describe the unfavorable condition that prevents the performance objective from being achieved.

- Reflect evidence found in data. This is not the place for opinions.

- Focus on only one issue per problem statement.

- Consist of clear, plain language—no educational jargon allowed.

- Provide answers for these questions:

  o Who does it impact?

  o What program, grade level or subject does it involve?

o Where is it occurring?

o When and/or how often is it occurring?

• Do not contain a cause or a solution.

The last bullet is perhaps the most difficult part of writing problem statements. We may want to quickly push to the end of the story, but it's not time yet. We cannot identify the best resolutions before we clearly unpack each problem down to the root cause or causes. If you skip the steps of finding the root cause(s), it is easy to make the mistake of designing a solution to address a contributing cause instead of a real root cause. The first step to identifying the root cause(s) is to write a clear, detailed problem statement. See Appendix C for a tool to help you clearly write a problem statement.

WHAT IS A ROOT CAUSE?

Have you ever had a problem that just refused to go away? You work and work on it, but it doesn't get resolved. The reason may be that you haven't yet discovered the root cause or all of the root causes. What is a root cause? Paul Preuss, in his book *School Leader's Guide to Root Cause Analysis,* defines a root cause as "the deepest underlying cause, or causes, of positive or negative symptoms within any process that, if dissolved, would result in elimination, or substantial reduction, of the symptom." (Preuss 2003, 3)

Often, when seeking a root cause, the easiest issue to identify is a symptom of the problem and not the root. For example, every year a high school had a very high ninth grade failure rate. After trying several strategies with little success, the district opted to open a ninth grade campus, thinking that isolating freshmen students on a campus of their own would eliminate the high failure rate. The new ninth grade campus was very expensive. It did reduce the failure rate for freshmen students, but interestingly, the failure rate for sophomores dramatically increased. The failure rate was a symptom of deeper issues and not the root cause of the problem.

Mark Paradies, president of System Improvements, works with businesses to investigate major accidents, manufacturing failures, etc.

He defines root cause as "the absence of a best practice or the failure to apply knowledge that would have prevented the problem." Paradies says that "people analyzing root causes are searching for best practices and knowledge to prevent problems. They aren't looking for people to blame or management failures. They are finding ways to perform work more reliably. This is a focus on improvement." (Paradies 2019)

Everyone gets frustrated with recurrent problems. Whether the problems are zombies, spam emails or weeds in your yard, when you can't stop something from coming back, frustration builds and our thinking often narrows. We sometimes jump to identify a solution based upon our past experiences or suggestions from colleagues. We just go for it. In our haste, we don't verify if we are addressing a root cause. Then, the problem returns, and we don't know why. If the problem is weeds, you can mow them or use an edger but you know they will come back. Spraying with weed killer may or may not work long term. You will experience immediate relief and see results—the weeds are gone! Sadly, the weeds will very likely return. Just like with returning zombies, the weeds often return bigger than ever before. To eliminate zombies, as you know, you have to destroy their brains. With weeds, you need to pull them out by the roots. And, with spam emails, I just say good luck. (There has to be a little humor inserted among all this talk about problems! And, zombies...they truly are imaginary. Please say I'm right!)

Did you notice that "roots" is plural? Weeds have more than one root. Some are larger and others are smaller just like problems in schools. Finding the most important root cause or causes can be complex. There are clusters of verifiable facts that contribute to any one problem in a school. Even if there are multiple reasons behind a problem, it's imperative that we seek the root causes. It may take time, and it may not be simple. But eliminating the root causes has the greatest impact on student learning.

CASTING THE FISHBONE'S WIDE NET

The purpose of the Fishbone activity is to brainstorm many contributing factors and causes of a problem. The fishbone throws a wide net to gather as much information as possible and visually places it together for a team to see how factors might be related or interact together. It is not the best tool for finding the root cause. School leaders often use this first to identify as many causes as possible, and then they use something like the Five Whys, discussed later in this chapter, to find the root cause(s).

Most fishbone templates organize the information by categories. The categories' subjects and the number of categories vary and are usually tailored to the problem. For example, if the problem is chronic absenteeism, the categories to explore might be (1) school climate, (2) student health, (3) lack of connectedness, (4) student behavior (5) academic need, and (6) family challenges. If the problem is low performance in 7th grade math, the categories might be (1) student engagement, (2) student mobility, (3) curriculum and materials, (4) instruction, and (5) professional learning.

A template is included later in this chapter (see Figure 6.6) and there are at least two easy ways to make a template yourself. The first option is for use with a small group. Simply take a piece of notebook paper and draw two vertical lines and one horizontal arrow to divide the paper into six equal sections. Write the problem to the left of the red notebook paper line. See Figure 6.1 for an example.

Figure 6.1 The Notebook Paper Fishbone

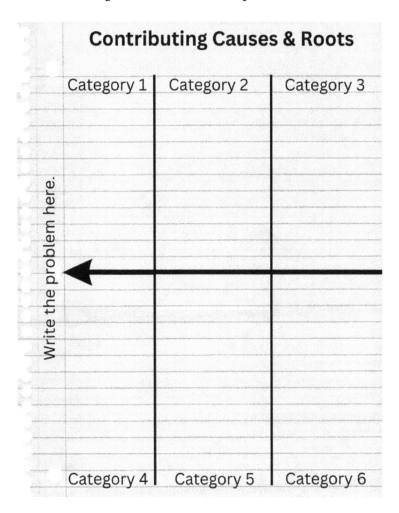

While it doesn't look like a fish, the template functions the same as those that do. Add the category titles and you are ready to record the contributing factors and causes as the team brainstorms.

A similar tool can be made with larger chart paper and sticky notes. Using this one works well if the team has a period of quiet thinking where each team member records ideas on sticky notes. Then, separately team members place their sticky notes under the correct category. Sticky notes with the same information are combined and layered. By layering the responses instead of removing duplicates, the team can see the impact of the cause. Offering quiet time for people to think on their own also prevents group-think where one opinion dominates the conversation and may not truly reflect all thinking.

FINDING THE ROOT CAUSE

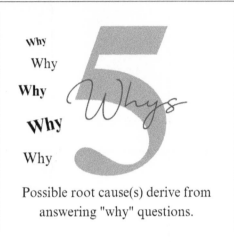

Possible root cause(s) derive from answering "why" questions.

There are several tools to help you identify the root cause and one of the simplest to use is the Five Whys. The process isn't 100% reliable, but many times it does work. Begin with a problem statement. With a team, brainstorm as many reasons for the problem as you can think of. There are no wrong answers and the more reasons you list, the more likely you will identify a root cause or causes. After brainstorming, ask the group to select one of the reasons on the list to explore more deeply. Then, the facilitator begins the Five Whys process by repeating the problem statement and asks why it is happening. Someone gives a response. The facilitator asks why the response is happening and receives another response. The sequence is repeated approximately five times or you receive a response, and the team agrees that it is a root cause. An example is included in Figure 6.2 below.

Figure 6.2 Five Whys - Example 1

The Five Whys

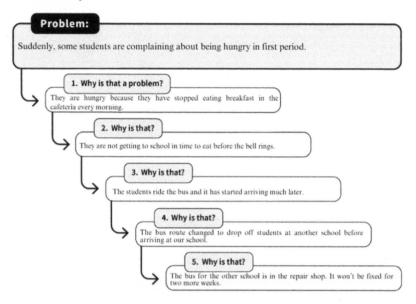

Problem:
Suddenly, some students are complaining about being hungry in first period.

1. Why is that a problem?
They are hungry because they have stopped eating breakfast in the cafeteria every morning.

2. Why is that?
They are not getting to school in time to eat before the bell rings.

3. Why is that?
The students ride the bus and it has started arriving much later.

4. Why is that?
The bus route changed to drop off students at another school before arriving at our school.

5. Why is that?
The bus for the other school is in the repair shop. It won't be fixed for two more weeks.

The staff can make temporary arrangements to allow the students to eat before going to class until the bus is fixed. Problem solved. If the last answer hadn't revealed that this is a temporary problem or if the answers had shown answers not in the school's control, then you need to take a step back in the process and investigate areas where the school does have control.

While it is true that some root causes are out of the school's control, there is still a bright spot to look for. Often more than one root cause exists. That fact is exactly what passionate educators need. Instead of giving up, look for other root causes that can be solved. Eliminating one root cause can even reduce the impact of other root causes or contributing causes.

Be aware that a cause that is out of the school's control can shut down the conversation. Figure 6.3 Example 2 below shows a response that does just that—it shuts down the conversation. You can't answer when it is out of the school's control.

Figure 6.3 The Five Whys - Example 2

The Five Whys

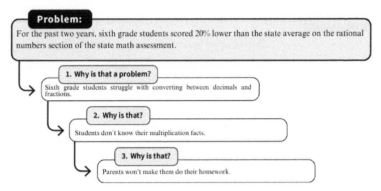

In this example, we have to stop. We have no control over whether parents make their children do homework or not. So, we go back to the problem statement and start again in Figure 6.4 below.

Figure 6.4 The Five Whys - Example 2 Revised

The Five Whys

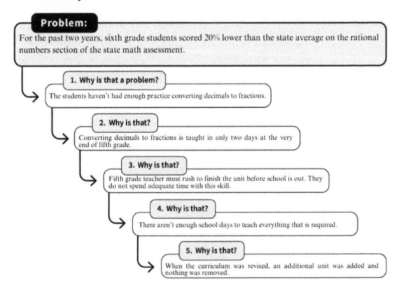

Now, we see a root cause that is within our control—the fifth grade math curriculum contains too many requirements, and the teachers don't have enough time to teach all of it.

Were you able to identify the contributing cause? If you said math fact fluency is the contributing cause, you're correct! In fact, most problem statements will have multiple contributing causes and may have more than one root cause. Identify as many as you can. Also, you may not get to the root cause with five questions. It may take three or it may take seven or eight. Keep going until you get an answer where everyone agrees it is the root or it doesn't make sense to look for more options.

A template for using the Five Whys is in Appendix D, but you really don't need one. Asking the question "why" is easy: it eliminates confusion, it is specific, and it doesn't take any special preparation.

After the Five Whys, if you find that you have several underlying causes and you aren't sure if they are root causes or contributing causes, try going just a little deeper with the flowchart in Figure 6.5.

Figure 6.5 Root Cause vs Contributing Cause

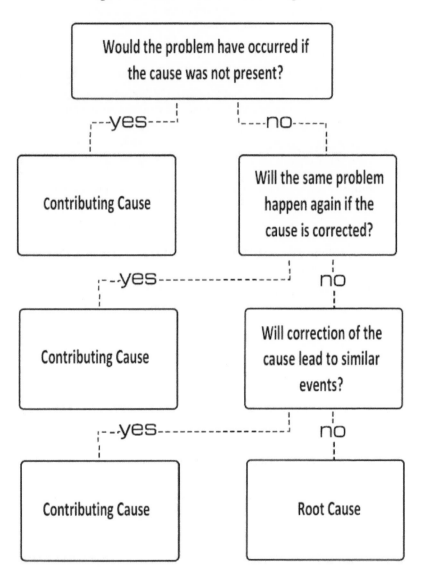

(Adapted from the University of Maryland Root Cause Analysis Facilitator Guide, 2019)

CHECK THE DIAL FISHBONE FOR THE ROOT CAUSE(S)

Some problems are extremely complex with no clear cut root cause. If you can't seem to get to the root of the problem, you probably have more than one. In this case, it is often helpful to take the fishbone structure discussed earlier in this chapter a little deeper. This time, you will list information about the possible root causes out together and consider how they are impacting each other.

There are four areas that frequently create a significant impact on learning. We call these four the DIAL. Dial stands for discipline, instruction, attendance, and language. There may be other factors included in the problem, but one or more of these big four are often involved. Strategies to eliminate problems in these four areas have the potential to make a weighty difference.

To use the DIAL Fishbone, list the problem on the fish's head. With a team, brainstorm factors from the four areas that could be causing at least part of the problem. Brainstorm as many as you can think of—there are no wrong answers. Then, step back and look at the picture as a whole. What factors could be working together, making the problem more complicated? For example, are there factors with instruction that are causing disciplinary issues, which are compounding the problem? Are language barriers causing poor attendance, which is widening the problem? If you go through your list and still haven't discovered the root causes, substitute other categories and keep brainstorming. Keep at it until your team begins to find areas where you need to explore and dig deeper into the data. Examples of other categories to consider include school climate, student health, connectedness, family challenges, student engagement, student mobility, curriculum/ materials, and professional learning. For more information on using the DIAL and next steps, see the guide in Appendix E.

Figure 6.6 The DIAL Fishbone

Brainstorm how the DIAL impacts the problem

Not all problems have DIAL causes, but many do. How might the big four cause or impact the problem?

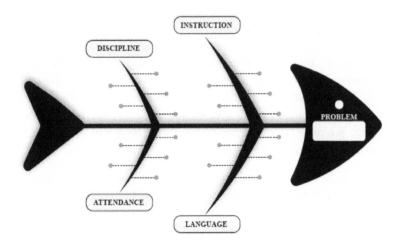

CIRCLE OF INFLUENCE

One way to help school leaders see their influence of control is to list the obstacles on a Circle of Influence. Based on Daniel Venables's research, here is how it works. Draw two circles, one inside the other. Add a label inside the largest circle as "Schools Can Influence." Label the smaller inner circle as "Schools Can Control." Outside the circles, label the area as "School Cannot Control." See Figure 6.7 as an example.

Figure 6.7 Circle of Influence

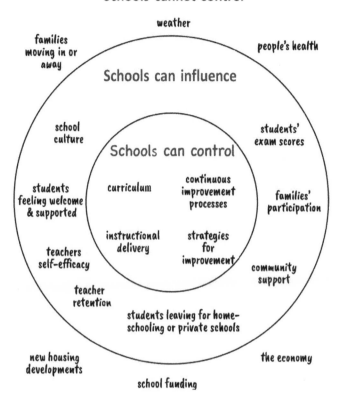

As your teams discuss obstacles, have them identify the amount of influence they have over the obstacle and write the name of the obstacle in the appropriate area. This activity helps validate challenges but also creates perspective. Focusing on areas over which we have no control shuts down the creative thinking necessary to solve problems for which we DO have some control or influence. "Even the most pessimistic teachers who claim the obstacles far outweigh their areas of influence can be reeled in by completing a Circle of Influence." (Venables 2014, 49–50) Sometimes using the power of influence works better than finding the root cause.

Working with middle schoolers is both a joy and a challenge. As a middle school principal, I would often shake my head and wonder where they get some of their ideas. One fall, a school-wide problem erupted that took more than finding the root cause. The problem was that for reasons unknown, the boys started wearing hairnets—the light, nylon hair nets that you often see in the food service industry. It wasn't just one race, ethnicity, or social group and no one could tell us why hairnets (that looked so silly) became a popular thing. The hairnets quickly became a problem because middle schoolers touch everything. Boys would yank one off someone's head, stretch it, and shoot it across the room like a rubber band. The hairnets were everywhere and then became the catalyst to arguments and fights. We tried everything to stop the behavior, including detentions, calling parents, etc. The faculty met together one afternoon to figure out a solution. We tried the Five Whys, seeking the root cause or causes for why the boys were wearing hairnets and produced these:

- Long hair, especially with bangs covering the eyes, was popular. Teachers regularly asked the boys to move their bangs away from their eyes. The hairnets kept their hair back.

- The weather was exceptionally warm that fall, staying in the high 90s for several weeks. The hairnets helped with the heat by keeping hair off their necks and off their foreheads when the boys were participating in athletics or physical education outside.

Neither of these reasons helped us think of a way to get them to stop wearing the hairnets and the rowdy behavior the hairnets caused.

Formulating a question in different ways can help you look at problems differently. Traditional disciplinary actions with individual students one at a time wasn't working. Instead of asking why the boys were wearing hairnets, we looked at the problem from a different angle. The question we asked was, "Is there a school-wide action we can take, impacting all students at the same time, which would make wearing a hairnet unpopular?" This led to a lively discussion and a list of ideas. One idea stood out, and we agreed to try it.

The next day, the entire faculty and staff wore hairnets. That's all it took. After just one day of teachers and staff sporting hairnets of our own, we never saw another hairnet on a student. Lesson learned? If you can't beat 'em, join 'em!

PRIORITIZING THE PROBLEMS

When continuous improvement teams analyze data, you can be sure that many problems will be revealed because that's what educators do—find problems and fix them! During the CNA process, teams often review too much data for fear of missing something. "School improvement teams need to understand that the critical task in the planning phase is to rule in the important data available to them while ruling out the inconsequential…otherwise the scope of team efforts will be too large, and the opportunity to focus on high-leverage improvement opportunities will be lost." (White and Smith 2010, 34) This is another reason why it is so important for the DOT to be the initial managers of data. When the analysis is complete and all the problems have been identified, the next step is to prioritize them so that the school can focus on the high-leverage improvement opportunities.

Sometimes prioritizing is easy. Other times, you may need a tool to help. Multi-voting is an easy method for narrowing the list of problem statements when the initial list is too long. The instructions for using multi-voting are included in Appendix F.

Why is prioritizing important? Not long ago I facilitated a planning meeting with district-level administrators in a large school district. Our purpose was to simplify the district's plan. The group had just completed a successful needs assessment snapshot process that involved additional stakeholders. The purpose was to inform the development of the continuous improvement plan for the upcoming school year. Everyone seemed pleased with the revealed strengths and identified needs. New goals had just been adopted, and the administrators were happy that the number was reduced from eight goals to four. That was a great start.

The next step was to rewrite the needs as problem statements and confirm that the root cause or causes developed during the previous meeting still sounded plausible. In groups of 4-5 people, most administrators worked on the problem statements that applied to their job descriptions, so they were able to complete the task with very few questions. The problem statements/root causes were recorded together in a Google document so everyone could see the entire list. I was excited to make so much progress rather quickly. But, that is where the easy part ended. The next task in simplifying the plan was to prioritize the problems or at least narrow the list down so that when they held the next continuous improvement Advisory Committee meeting with additional stakeholders, they wouldn't be trying to sort through a list of 60+ problem statements.

To start the prioritizing process, I conducted a short presentation on fragmentation citing the work of Dr. Douglas Reeves from his book *Deep Change Leadership*. Dr. Reeves says this:

> In a study I conducted of more than two thousand school plans, I evaluated the relationship between the number of priorities educational leaders attempted to implement and their gains or losses in student achievement over three years. (Reeves 2016) The analysis included students in elementary, middle, and high school grades and all academic disciplines, including literacy, mathematics, science, and social studies. The results were dramatic. Schools with six or fewer priorities had dramatically higher gains than those with more initiatives. Indeed, my colleagues and I found individual schools with more than 70 priorities and education systems with more than 240 priorities. (Reeves 2016) The conclusion was striking: more than six priorities was inversely proportional to gains in performance. The first few priorities allow for focus by leaders, employees, and the entire organization. But after six priorities, it became impossible to monitor implementation, and both leaders and employees lose focus. (Reeves 2021, 78)

Sometimes you can feel the tone change in a room, and as I finished my presentation, I could feel it. By the looks on their faces, I could see that this would be a big shift in the way they had done things in the past. Dropping from 60+ problem statements down to no more than six? How could that work in a large district? I asked them to refill their coffee and then in small groups, look at last year's problem statements and the corresponding performance objectives. I wanted them to see if they could categorize the performance objectives into one of these three groups:

1. **Compliance requirements**—things mandated by local, state, or federal requirements. These are often things that require some sort of documentation for audit purposes.

2. **Job description expectations**—things that the district expects professional educators to do as part of their everyday job requirements.

3. **Continuous improvement objectives**—things that point directly to the district's goals and will help propel the district toward achieving their vision.

As I walked around the room, I could hear some "aha moments." All the things they identified as problem statements were valid and important. However, not everything that is important rises to the level of a priority for the district's continuous improvement plan.

We expect all educators to follow the law. I asked them to consider moving the compliance pieces somewhere else so that the focus in the CIP could be on the most important priorities. When the law requires documentation in the plan, use a software product, such as Plan4Learning, to create a separate section at the back for compliance items. Sometimes operational procedures are required. Those, too, can be grouped at the back in a separate section or addendum. Job descriptions, program rules, maps, school calendars, and other operational information are better addressed in locations other than the CIP. By minimizing what goes in the plan, the CIP has a greater opportunity to create focus and clarity about the district's priorities.

As they talked, they also considered these questions for each problem statement:

1. Who is impacted by this problem?

2. How big and how widespread is the problem?

3. How important is the problem to achieving the district's goals?

   • How will student outcomes be improved?

   • How will teacher efficacy be increased?

   • How will organizational systems be improved?

4. What is anticipated to happen if this problem is NOT removed?

5. How feasible is it to address this problem?

- Do we have access to the needed resources, including time?

- Do we have available staff or can capacity be developed/recruited?

- Will the staff support it?

- Can the problem be addressed by the effective selection and implementation of evidence-based practices? Can we build upon something already in place?

6. Are there other problems that rank above this one that should be addressed first?

The conversations were hard. Some directors of programs felt that the schools would not comply if their program's rules were not included in the plan. As we continued to talk, people began to think differently about what should go into the plan. By the end of the meeting, we had whittled the list down to 19 problem statements for the Continuous Improvement Advisory Committee to consider. That was still too many, but a more manageable number for the committee to consider and prioritize.

What a victory! A smaller number of prioritized problem statements is a huge step toward simplifying the continuous improvement plan. This paves the way to developing performance objectives and the strategies, which will be explored in Chapters 7 and 8. See how these work together to complete the continuous improvement plan components in Figure 6.8 below.

Figure 6.8 Continuous Improvement Components

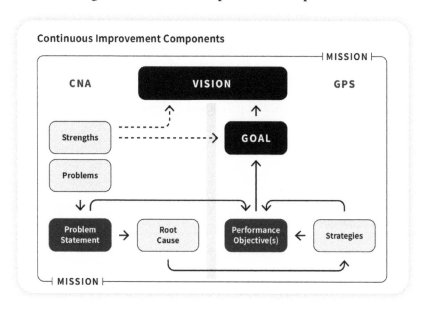

Notice in the graphic that there is a gray line dividing the continuous improvement planning process into two components. Everything to the left of the line is part of the comprehensive needs assessment. The end of this chapter completes our learning about what it takes to create the CNA. The CNA is powerful, and when done well, it is the propulsion for the second part of the plan, the GPS. Both parts are equally important to the continuous improvement planning cycle.

STRESS RELIEF: GOING DEEPER WITH THE ROOT CAUSE QUESTIONS

If you have tried more than one round of the Five Whys and used the DIAL Fishbone and still can't determine the root cause(s), walk away for a while. When you're ready to start again, try using these questions to guide and and inspire new thinking:

1. How did you discover the problem?

    a. What is the evidence that confirms it is a problem and not an assumption?

   b. What are the symptoms leading up to the problem? Do the symptoms point to part of the root cause(s)?

2. What conditions allow the problem to occur?

   a. Why do the conditions allow the problem?

   b. Are the conditions permanent or temporary?

   c. Who is contributing to the problem? How and why?

3. What systems interact with the problem? How?

   a. Does instruction or the curriculum contribute to the problem?

   b. Does the school schedule or time contribute?

   c. Do school rules or policies contribute to the problem?

   d. Do adults (teachers, staff, families) contribute to the problem?

4. What is missing that contributes to the problem?

   a. Does the problem have to do with adult training or planning?

   b. Is there a lack of materials, technology, equipment, or facilities?

   c. Is something not being implemented correctly?

5. Has someone not involved with the problem analyzed the data?

Chapter 7

GOALS AND
PERFORMANCE OBJECTIVES

> *"Goals transform a random walk into a chase."*
> *Mihaly Csikszentmihalyi*

American psychologist Mihaly Csikszentmihalyi studied thousands of people and concluded that our obsessive focus on goals for a good life, money, an important job, etc. have led us astray. Achieving these things do not create happiness, and they deflect our thinking away from what truly matters. He says that happiness is achieved within ourselves. The best goals are those that require a high degree of skill and commitment without creating excessive anxiety and pressure. (Csikszentmihalyi 2008) I believe the same principle applies in continuous improvement.

In a school context, achieving a goal of 5% higher scores in reading will not create a school's happiness or success. Sure, it might help the school get off the low-performing list, but the "happiness" that it produces is short-term. Our goals must have deeper meaning and impact. The goal of having every student reading on grade level is much more meaningful. Goals need to propel us toward achieving our vision. A simple structure for ensuring the use of impact goals is the GPS which is an acronym for **g**oals, **p**erformance objectives, and **s**trategies.

WHAT IS THE GPS?

Because there are so many complexities to planning, it makes sense to use the simplest, most streamlined format possible in a one-year continuous improvement plan (CIP). There are two sections in a CIP. The first is the CNA, and the second section is for the **g**oals, **p**erformance objectives, and **s**trategies. The acronym created by using the first letter of each component is GPS. That is quite fitting because this section is where all the actions take place. The GPS section of the CIP is created using the results of the most current CNA snapshot—the strengths and prioritized problems with their root causes. Before we go deeper, let's define the three components of the GPS:

Goal—A goal is a powerful direction-altering achievement that typically takes more than one year to accomplish. In this GPS format, three or four goals are set at the district level and are included in every school's plan. While the schools' plans are uniquely developed to address the results of their CNA snapshots, it is still important that school plans also address the district's goals. This is to ensure there is alignment and cohesiveness across the district from Pre-Kindergarten through 12th grade. This requirement doesn't typically cause a problem because the district goals reflect the findings in the district's CNA snapshot, which includes data from each school. So, the district's areas for focus, and the schools' areas for focus are usually the same.

Because the district goals are addressed in each school's plan, the goal-setting process should not be taken lightly. These goals shape the entire district's continuous improvement efforts for more than one year, so careful thought must go into *how* they are written. James Clear, author of the book *Atomic Habits*, offers an explanation that can help prevent school leaders from making the mistake of setting goals that are short-sighted or short-term. He says, "Goals are for people who care about winning once. Systems are for people who care about winning repeatedly." (Clear 2018) Clear goes on to explain that when an athlete prepares to run in a race, her goal shouldn't be to win. A better goal is to become an exceptional, life-long runner. Clear says that the race is a short-term target that lets the athlete know if she is on track to becoming an exceptional runner. (Clear 2018) Taking that perspective, let's again revisit the goal of increasing reading scores by 5%. This is common language in goals, but using Clear's guidelines, we now see this is a short-term target. Wording like this is much better in a performance objective. Performance objectives usually span about one school year. A true goal stretches beyond the short-term and seeks a greater impact. A better goal, then, is for students to become proficient, literate readers.

Use the acronym "BOLD" to help you remember the characteristics of strong, vision-bound goals.

- **B = broad:** Goals are written at the conceptual level and should be BIG and inspiring. A truly bold goal goes beyond compliance and might be incapable of being measured in quantifiable units. Goals are major milestones toward the long-term desires for students' success and should courageously press toward the school's vision.

- **O = outcome-based:** Goals are based on the desired end results or the impact of achievement. Goals drive toward transformation. You can visualize the momentousness of achieving the vision through a well-articulated goal.

- **L = long-term:** Goals contain innovation and inspire boundless growth. They are challenging and can't be achieved overnight. Most goals span 3-5 years or maybe longer. They accelerate the mission and bring the vision into full view for the district.

- **D = district-level:** In districts with strong GPS continuous improvement alignment, the goals are district-level and provide clear direction for all schools. However, because of their format, the goals also allow school plans to uniquely align to the details of their needs assessments. In other words, all schools address their distinctive needs through performance objectives and strategies.

Here are some examples of BOLD district goals:

- Support and equip all students through caring professionals delivering high-quality programming and sound educational experiences for all students.

- Provide a rigorous and relevant curriculum and deliver

instruction that is responsive to the needs of all students.

- Foster active parent and family engagement through meaningful opportunities for relationship building, participation, feedback, and collaboration.

- Attract, develop, retain, and reward highly effective teachers in an environment where talented staff and students feel valued and supported.

Performance Objective—A performance objective (PO) measures progress toward achieving a large goal. It breaks the BOLD goal down to a short-term target to achieve this school year. A PO helps the school stay on-track. The business world calls it a key performance indicator or KPI. A well-written PO follows the SMARTER acronym, an expanded version of the SMART (specific, measurable, achievable, realistic, and time-bound) acronym. SMARTER will be defined later in this chapter. While the goals are all the same for each school in the district, the POs are unique for each school because they are based upon the prioritized problems identified during the CNA snapshot process. There are typically one to three POs per goal with the following characteristics. Performance objectives:

- Measure a school's progress toward achieving an associated goal by describing how much the school anticipates it can grow in one year.

- Offer a sense of achievement and motivates school leaders to work towards big goals.

- Link the CNA snapshot to the GPS because the POs are a direct reflection of the prioritized problem statements.

- Provide focus for the strategies through the root cause(s) associated with each prioritized problem statement.

Here are some examples of performance objectives:

- On the EOY Example Assessment administered in May, 85% of Kindergarten-2nd grade students will score "On/Above Grade Level."

- By June 20___, student performance on Grades 6-8 state exams will increase in all subjects tested by at least 3 points at each performance level (approaches, meets, masters).

- On the student survey administered in May 20___, the percent of students in grades 9-12 who report feeling connected as both individuals and learners will be at least 3 percentage points higher than last year's survey results.

- By December 20___, 100% of 11th graders will have a documented preliminary post-secondary plan.

Strategy - A strategy contains powerful and targeted action steps that describe how the PO will be accomplished. It may take more than one strategy to successfully achieve the PO. Strategies follow the *BEST* format and will be fully defined in the next chapter.

See a picture of the GPS components in Figure 7.1.

Figure 7.1 The GPS

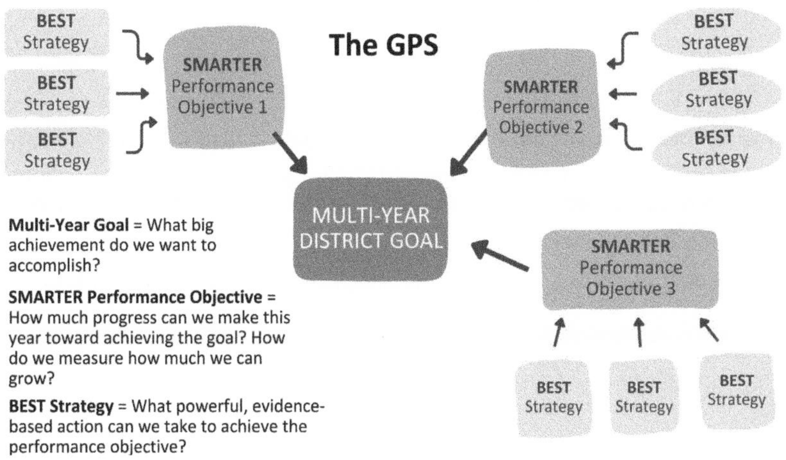

Multi-Year Goal = What big achievement do we want to accomplish?

SMARTER Performance Objective = How much progress can we make this year toward achieving the goal? How do we measure how much we can grow?

BEST Strategy = What powerful, evidence-based action can we take to achieve the performance objective?

GOALS AND PERFORMANCE OBJECTIVES—WHY BOTH?

Among the most highly debated planning terms—sometimes even used interchangeably—are *goal* and *objective*. If we take a quick look at the meaning of both words, it is easy to see why. Both words involve growth and achievement. However, as we see in the descriptions above, there are significant differences. A goal represents the big picture: the ultimate outcome you intend to achieve. Performance objectives are the specific smaller targets that lead to achieving the big goal. Goals and performance objectives work in tandem, and you need both. The clearer you are with the goal, the more likely you are to succeed. But goals can be overwhelming and without the shorter-term, measurable performance objectives, your school might not ever achieve the goal.

Think of it like this: If you want to see Palo Duro Canyon, the second largest canyon in the United States, your goal is to get to the canyon. Next, you will need to determine how you're going to get there and decide how you will know if you are on the right road and making progress. That is your performance objective. If you only focus on the goal of reaching Palo Duro Canyon without considering making progress on the right road, it's likely that time will pass, and you will remain in the same location. If you only focus on your mode of transportation without being clear about exactly where Palo Duro Canyon is, you might end up in Amarillo, Texas. Amarillo isn't far from the canyon, but it isn't *in* the canyon. You won't reach your goal. To prevent these problems, it is important to know both your end destination (the goal) and if your mode of transportation is helping you make the amount of progress (performance objective) you need to get there. The goal provides direction while the performance objective measures your progress toward following the direction.

CREATING THE DISTRICT GOALS

Where do the district goals come from? The district follows the same CNA snapshot process that the schools do, and if a district strategic plan is in place, the district will use both the CNA snapshot and the strategic plan to set new goals. Remember, district goals often span more than one year, and they may not contain all of the typical SMART components.

The end-of-year evaluation and the CNA snapshot process will confirm if the district goals will stay in place or need to be revised.

SOAR TO NEW HEIGHTS WITH GOALS

One reason why some people don't embrace continuous improvement planning is that so much of the work centers on what is wrong or what is missing. It is true that a needs assessment can reinforce a deficit mindset. However, there is a growing movement to build a CIP based upon opposite factors—the assets of the school. This movement accentuates the areas where the school excels. The asset-based approach finds good things in the school and community that often go untapped and builds upon those. One option that aligns with the asset-based, capacity building approach is to conduct a SOAR analysis.

SOAR is an acronym for Strengths, Opportunities, Aspirations, and Results. This planning process utilizes a school's or district's strengths to help your team recognize potential and design lofty but relevant goals. Using this planning tool with your stakeholders can inspire them to engage in the highly valued pursuit of excellence and growth. Because it is focused on strengths instead of the usual focus on deficiencies, SOAR also helps generate innovative, out-of-the-box thinking. The template is a four quadrant matrix highlighting Strengths, Opportunities, Aspirations, and Results. See Figure 7.2.

Figure 7.2 SOAR Questions

Goal/Performance Objective Setting Activity

STRENGTHS
What can we build on?

1. What are we most proud of as a school? How does that reflect our greatest strengths?
2. What makes us unique when compared to others?
3. In what areas can we be the best in education?
4. How do we use our strengths to get results?
5. What do we provide that is exemplary for students, staff and other stakeholders?

OPPORTUNITIES
What are our stakeholders asking for?

1. What are the top 3 opportunities on which we should focus our efforts?
2. How can we best meet the needs of our students, staff and other stakeholders?
3. How can we distinctively differentiate ourselves from others?
4. How can we reframe challenges to be seen as exciting opportunities?
5. What new skills do we need to move us forward?

SOAR

ASPIRATIONS
What is our preferred future?

1. When we explore our values and aspirations, what are we deeply passionate about?
2. Reflecting on our vision, mission, values, strengths and opportunities, who are we now? Who should we become? Where should we go in the future?
3. What are our most compelling aspirations?
4. What strategic initiatives (strategies, processes, programs) will support our aspirations?

RESULTS
How will we know when we have achieved our vision?

1. Considering our strengths, opportunities, and aspirations, what 3-5 meaningful measures will indicate that we are on track to achieving our vision?
2. What are the most important steps to take in order to achieve our vision?
3. What resources are needed to implement the most vital initiatives of our vision?
4. What will be different for our students, staff, and other stakeholders?

To use the SOAR model, follow these steps:

1. Schedule a goal-setting session with your Advisory Committee. A good time to do this is after a CNA data analysis session.

2. Using the top row of the SOAR matrix, answer the questions and fill in the squares. The top row reflects the present. The strengths box represents things that are internal—the strengths the school has today. The opportunities box represents things that are external—what are students, families, staff asking for? What is it they see in other schools that they want for us? These are tangible benefits and advantages that the school can achieve—not wild dreams.

3. Using the bottom rows, answer the questions and fill in the squares. The bottom row reflects the future. The aspirations box represents future objectives and intentions. This is where you challenge the status quo and innovate towards new ideas. It's something fresh and challenging. The results box represents the measurable results that show improved performance. In other words, these become goals if you are doing this at the district level or the performance objectives if you are doing this at a school. See Appendix G for a blank SOAR template.

The SOAR process is a really different approach. It's the exact opposite of the more commonly used SWOT analysis which stands for strengths, weaknesses, opportunities and threats. SOAR's benefit is to confirm that current goals are heading in the right direction—they are pointing toward the vision. Answering the SOAR questions and holding a discussion with stakeholders can be a positive, uplifting experience. The downside to it is that it can lack granularity and detail. It may not contain enough information for some schools to be able to build strategies. If a school has spent multiple years in school improvement, it can feel like every conversation is negative. SOAR can bring in a positive perspective and find something worth celebrating. It might even be used in conjunction with one or two deficit-based strategies to create balance. The SOAR process isn't just limited to goal setting. It can be used to explore, focus or redirect initiatives, or to jumpstart something new. SOAR is a great way to build upon strengths and identify assets. The following example is a powerful story about SOARing to success.

Many Dallas Cowboy football fans would agree that former running back, Emmitt Smith, was an outstanding football player. His list of accomplishments is long, and his strengths are innumerable. However, Emmitt Smith also had deficiencies. Early in his career, his small stature and speed were marked as the qualities that would most likely prevent him from playing at higher levels. But by building upon his strengths, his assumed weaknesses quickly became irrelevant. Emmitt has three Super Bowl rings, a Super Bowl MVP award, and a seat in the Hall of Fame to prove that focusing on strengths works. Some schools spend so much time focusing on deficiencies that they fail to utilize their strengths as a means for moving them toward effective change. If Emmitt had done that, his football career might have been drastically different. Look for the strengths you can build on, opportunities you can take advantage of, aspirations you would like to achieve and the results that will measure your accomplishments. SOAR with your planning.

SMARTER PERFORMANCE OBJECTIVES

The SMART acronym and process for formatting goals has been around for many years. Most educators know it so well they can say the words associated with the acronym without even thinking. But keep reading for a new perspective. SMARTER adds a call to action that brings new life to the time-tested acronym. In the GPS, goals are district-level. They are broad, multiyear, and written at the conceptual level, which may be difficult to measure. This is where we want them to be because worthy and direction-altering goals take time and are difficult to accomplish. They don't always fit the widely-accepted SMART goals structure. The associated performance objectives (POs) *do* fit the SMART structure and should be written that way with some adjustments.

One problem with the SMART acronym is that it is just a statement with no call to action. Without action, you simply have words on a page. A PO with nothing to propel it into action may not get accomplished. Even worse, it might not be noticed until the end of the year when it is too late. To make a plan effective, there must be a way to know if progress is occurring throughout the year and also an evaluation of effectiveness at the end of the year. A solution is to upgrade and expand

SMART to SMARTER. The "E" and the "R" stand for evaluated and reviewed, respectively. Adding these components creates a PO the desired call to action. Additionally, SMARTER moves beyond just an objective. It becomes a measure that requires movement toward continuous improvement. SMARTER POs are described in Figure 7.3.

Figure 7.3 SMARTER Performance Objective (PO) Acronym

SMARTER PERFORMANCE OBJECTIVES

S	Specific with a Stretch, Significant	Who is involved? What behaviors, skills, knowledge, and programs are addressed? Does the PO push beyond the status quo? Does it answer when, where, which, how, and/or why? Is it detailed and exact so that the risk of misinterpretation is minimized?
M	Measurable, Meaningful, Motivating	How is progress measured? Does growth in this area currently make sense? Is there an established baseline? What criteria or degree of growth will be used to identify success?
A	Achievable, Agreed-Upon, Ambitious, Aligned	Is the desired outcome possible? Does the PO reflect an aggressive move to close the achievement gap or increase the strengths? Is it challenging? Does it require effort? Do people accept this challenge? Is it equitable, appropriate and aligned?
R	Relevant and Reasonable to the goal, Results-based	Does achieving the PO press the school toward achieving the district's goal and the school's vision for excellence? Is it aligned with state and federal standards? Does it increase equitable opportunities?
T	Timely, Tied, Trackable	Does it make sense to focus on this PO now? Is the PO tied to the CNA with a clear relationship with the most critical problems or prioritized strengths? Can we track progress? Do we have a clear picture of the desired amount of progress for the year?
E	Evaluated	What is the expected impact? How will we measure success and how will we know if a change is an improvement? When will the final evaluation for the year occur? Who needs to be involved? Are all of these clearly defined before implementation of the PO begins?
R	Reviewed	Are status checks scheduled approximately every 9 weeks to measure progress? Is the amount of measurable progress needed for each 9-weeks clearly defined so that the PO will be achieved? Who is involved? Are personnel empowered to make needed adjustments to the PO's associated strategies as soon as they are identified? How are changes in actions communicated to the school?

Adding the "R"call to action in SMARTER performance objectives brings the distant end-of-the-year evaluation closer by establishing 90-day reviews to check the status and measure progress. These 90-day reviews make the performance objective more meaningful, especially if you create a timeline identifying how much progress is needed each 90-day period so that the PO can be achieved. Shannon, a high school assistant principal, says that she creates a simple table to help her team calculate how much progress they think they can achieve each 90-calendar days. Her school monitors their plan four times during the year. The school is on a 9-week grading system, so it makes it easy to think about the school year in four quarters. In her table, she first counts the number of instructional days for each quarter. Then, she subtracts days for special events, district and state testing, and any other potential reason why instruction might be disrupted for large numbers of students. With a revised number of instructional days to consider, Shannon says that it makes it easier to set progress measures for each quarter.

It's not a perfect system, but she finds that they can more accurately set their desired growth than they could when they simply divided the needed growth into four even percentages. Shannon adds that the table also creates an unintended benefit. It creates a healthy sense of urgency to not waste a single instructional day. Shannon used to use the term "90-day monitoring reviews", but she found it to be misleading on their school calendar. There may be 90 days if you include Saturdays and Sundays, but when you look at the actual number of instructional days available, it's less than half. When you put the real number out there, people are often shocked at how little time is available. Figure 7.4 is a look at Shannon's table:

Figure 7.4 Shannon's Quarterly Progress Planning Table

Quarterly Progress Planning	1st Quarter/ Formative	2nd Quarter/ Formative	3rd Quarter/ Formative	4th Quarter/ Summative
DATES	Aug 8 – Oct 4	Oct 10 – Dec 15	Jan 2 – Mar 8	Mar 18 – May 22
Number of instructional Days in School Calendar	40	44	44	44
List the number of instructional days that will be disrupted due to special events.	Homecoming - 2 College Fair - 1 District Exam - 1	Early Release - 1 EOC Exam - 5 School Play - 1	Pre-Registration - 1 Field Test - 2	Early Release - 1 State Exam - 5 Academic Meet - 2 Grad. Practice - 1
Adjusted Number of Instructional Days	36	37	41	35

When setting the performance objectives (POs), remember to address the needs of all student groups not meeting expected levels of performance or growth. If several student groups are targeted for specific growth, you can use a small table at the end of the PO for clarity. For example, if one student group needs to grow 3% and another student group needs to grow 2%, you can designate those differences in your table.

The list of prioritized problem statements from the CNA snapshot provides the content, context, and justification for the POs. Not each CNA problem statement needs its own PO because sometimes two or three problem statements can be addressed within one PO. Because each PO is supported by strategies, you will want a limited number of POs to keep your plan at a manageable size. After you draft the performance objectives, double-check to be sure they represent all of the prioritized problems and any prioritized strengths. What gets measured, gets done. Your POs are your measurements.

Achieving POs should require effort. They usually aren't easy to achieve, but they are attainable. It requires "work with a stretch." Dr. David Dockterman, professor at Harvard's Graduate School of Education, says that productive struggle and a learning mindset fuel innovation and growth. "As you set goals for yourself and others, use stories of struggle-to-success as reminders that achieving difficult goals is hard work, often involving many failures along the way. Setting the expectation for the ups and downs of learning can help sustain the belief in the possibility of success." (Dockterman 2017) One way to help draft a PO that is a productive struggle is to place it next to the priority problem(s) it is designed to address. See Figure 7.5 below and then consider the following three questions:

- Why does this problem matter and for whom?

- What are the consequences for NOT eliminating the problem this year?

- Does the performance objective align with the energy of our mission, providing a call to action with a challenging stretch?

Figure 7.5 Priority Problems and SMARTER POs

Priority Problem Statement:
The English Learners / Emergent Bilinguals consistently score at least 10% or more below all other student groups at all grade levels on the state assessment.

SMARTER Performance Objective (PO):
By August of next year, our school will design and open a district-approved Kindergarten and 1st grade two-way dual language program.

Priority Problem Statement:
In three years, the failure rate for 9th graders in Algebra 1 has dropped 10 % in the all students group and 17 % in the special education student group.

SMARTER Performance Objective (PO):
This year's 9th grade state assessment scores will show Algebra 1 passing rates at least 5 % higher than last year in all student groups and the gap between special education and non-special education student groups will be reduced by at least 4 %.

Priority Problem Statement:
Student office referrals for discipline increased by 8 % in grades 4-5 as compared with last year's data.

SMARTER Performance Objective (PO):
This year, student office referrals for discipline will be reduced by 10 % in grades 4-5 and by at least 3 % in all other grade levels when compared with last year's data.

Before we reflect back on the three questions, did you notice that the first problem statement is not measured by student growth? Designing and implementing a dual language program represents a transformational change in instructional delivery. It is big with many strategies and action steps. Change of this magnitude is best addressed first at the PO level. The opening of the classrooms makes it measurable the first year. The following years will include student achievement.

So, how did you do with the three questions? Did you see that all of the problems listed in Figure 7.5 have big gaps that are urgent to close, and they have consequences for not closing them in one year? Sometimes simply answering those three questions is enough to set the measurable level of the PO. Other times, you may have to dig deeper in order to set the level of desired growth for the upcoming year. Six questions, adapted from the work of Anthony Bryk, Louis Gomez, Alicia Grunow and Paul LeMahieu, may help:

1. What has historically been the level of performance for this problem?

2. What has been typical performance in other schools that are similar to us?

3. What does exemplary performance in this area look like?

4. What is the goal associated with this performance objective?

5. What conditions unique to our school are likely to affect our performance?

6. What would be an appropriate stretch performance objective (challenging but also attainable) for this school year? (Bryk et. al, 2015, 152)

ALIGN GOALS AND PERFORMANCE OBJECTIVES WITH THE GPS

By now, you should have a good understanding of the relationship between goals and performance objectives. It's pretty straight forward, right? Both are needed, and the GPS keeps things simple. There are many different versions of continuous improvement planning, each with its own format and vocabulary. Trying to compare them can quickly become a Tower of Babel problem. It is confusing. However, almost all planning structures have a GPS in their format. It may be labeled with different terms, but if you understand the GPS structure with the big multi-year goal, followed by the more specific and measurable performance objective and then strategies, you can identify these essential planning components in almost any planning structure. Knowing where the GPS is will help you make sense of the functions in other continuous improvement structures. When looking at other continuous improvement planning structures, one question to ask is, "Why add extra layers of operations and terms that can be confusing when all you need is the GPS?"

From a district perspective, the GPS structure helps you see how the actions of all schools impact district results. It builds unity of purpose at each school and across the district. Instead of operating as a collection of schools, each with its own independent priorities, the GPS aligns all schools' improvement efforts with the district's priorities through the goals. Then, schools personalize how they will reach the district's goal according to their own unique needs. So, the performance objectives and strategies are different for each school. When a district's continuous improvement planning structure follows the GPS format, the school's plan becomes useful and relevant because it is aligned with the school's *real* work.

Without the GPS structure, a school often builds a plan stuffed full of meaningless strategies that are included just to fill in the blank spots in a confusing planning document. The GPS allows each school to address district-level goals in personalized ways that make sense for their school. In Figure 7.6 below, an elementary school PO addresses the district's multi-year goal of a 100% graduation rate. The use of SMARTER performance objectives allows the school to appropriately address the goal.

Figure 7.6 Elementary School PO Addressing a District Goal

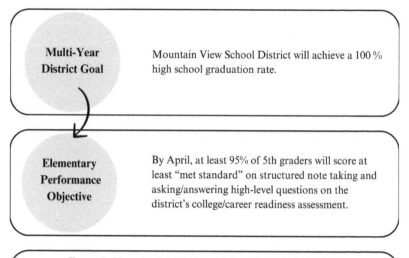

Multi-Year District Goal	Mountain View School District will achieve a 100 % high school graduation rate.
Elementary Performance Objective	By April, at least 95% of 5th graders will score at least "met standard" on structured note taking and asking/answering high-level questions on the district's college/career readiness assessment.

Example How the School Can Address the District's Goal

Strategies include training on two prioritized college/career readiness skills:
- asking/answering quality questions
- structured note-taking.

Mastery of these builds a foundation for academic habits students need for success in middle and high school.

If the district did not follow the GPS format, the elementary school might set strategies for a kindergarten graduation that won't have as strong an impact on high school graduation rates. Also, a high school that is several percentage points away from reaching 100% can realistically align with the district goal by designing two to three performance objectives that address specific graduation problems identified in the CNA process. One example is shown in Figure 7.7 below.

Figure 7.7 High School PO Addressing a District Goal

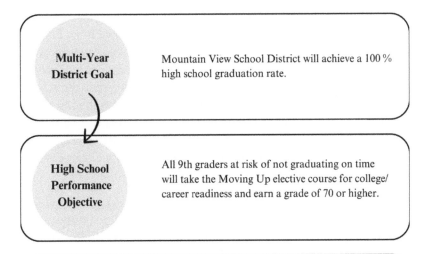

Multi-Year District Goal	Mountain View School District will achieve a 100 % high school graduation rate.
High School Performance Objective	All 9th graders at risk of not graduating on time will take the Moving Up elective course for college/career readiness and earn a grade of 70 or higher.

Example How the School Can Address the District's Goal

Objectives for students to master in the Moving Up elective include:

- develop a career plan with goals
- learn how to advocate for yourself
- learn how to receive feedback
- research college/career requirements
- complete the FAFSA application
- master five study habits
- develop critical thinking skills
- self-monitor grades

As we learned in Chapters 1 and 2, to produce transformation in schools, all planning should begin with the vision and mission. This is where focus begins. Another important benefit is that this focus will prevent the development of goals that impede the continuous improvement process. While not every single action conducted in a school is included in the CIP, the POs and strategies that are included have connections to the vision and mission. Continuous improvement planning focuses on systems and processes that produce positive effects on student learning. Every part of the GPS represents a collective voice around creating and growing an effective learning environment.

FOCUS ACTIONS WITH THE GPS

When school leaders say they don't see the benefit of using a continuous improvement plan, I go right to their plan's goals to see how they are written. Almost always they are not using the GPS format and the goals lack meaning. Where I expect to see a GPS, I often find generic words without the detail needed to inform educators about what the school is trying to achieve. The plan is not inspiring nor does it address the anticipated impact. For a continuous improvement plan to be useful, the GPS needs to begin with clearly written goals that reflect the vision. The goals will inspire a call to action for school leaders and energize the mission.

When a district goal is set to "increase the percentage of students meeting standards in grade 4 reading by 5%," the results can be measured, but this language provides little direction for the schools. It doesn't help the school know what processes are necessary to achieve the goal. This is an outcome-based goal. Very little additional information can be gleaned. But what if the goal contains more of an inspiring story about the system as a whole? Look at this district goal:

> The district will support and be responsive to the unique learning needs of all students through high-quality programming and sound educational experiences.

Now we have more knowledge about what the district desires to accomplish with its goal. We can go to our school's CNA snapshot and align problem statements with this goal. We will convert problem statements into performance objectives that we believe will help the district achieve this goal. Here is an example of what that might look like:

> **District Goal:** Support and be responsive to the unique learning needs of all students through high-quality programming and sound educational experiences.

> **School Problem Statement:** Emergent Bilinguals in our sheltered instruction program are consistently scoring 10-15% below our non-Emergent Bilinguals on the district benchmark assessments and the state exams.

School Performance Objective: In May, 20__, our school will close the achievement gap between Emergent Bilinguals and non-Emergent Bilinguals by at least 5% on the state exams while increasing the performance for all student groups by at least 3%.

In this example, the school is able to use information from the needs assessment about the performance of their Emergent Bilinguals. They create a PO that addresses the district goal. So, the school is able to address their unique needs with Emergent Bilinguals AND align their work with the district's goal. It is a win-win for both. The next step for the school will be to create strategies for the Emergent Bilinguals to accelerate their learning.

Reflecting back, if the original format of the district goal had been used, ("increase the percentage of students meeting standards in grade 4 reading by 5%") the school *might* align the Emergent Bilinguals' performance problem to the goal, but they might not see the connection. It probably depends on the number of Emergent Bilinguals in the 4th grade or other factors. It wouldn't be as easy to align the school's needs and the district's desired goal. Additionally, when you see one goal to "increase reading by 5%," you'll likely see the same thing repeated with mathematics, science, and other areas. The result is a very large, disconnected document lacking the story of a school's path toward transformation. This kind of plan is doomed to reside on a dusty bookshelf or be tucked away in a never-opened folder on the principal's computer.

MEASURING PROGRESS QUARTERLY

One reason why some improvement plans fail is the huge amount of time between the plan's creation and final evaluation. Plans are created in the spring or summer, months before the school year begins, and the final or summative evaluations will not occur until the following spring or summer - a year later. That is a very long time to stay on track. What if growth isn't happening? We sure don't want an entire year to go by before we discover what we're doing isn't working. That's where the word "continuous" becomes important. Goals and performance objectives are set and confirmed at the beginning of the school year and then evaluated at the end. It's what happens between those two dates that creates the continuous improvement journey. Continuous improvement is the path that professional educators take as we learn how our actions impact student learning. We use data so we know where to begin and then design the very best instruction possible. After we implement it for about 90 calendar days or 3 months, we analyze our progress so we can make adjustments, if needed, before going further. As John Hattie says:

> It is to know thy impact, it is to understand this impact, and it is to act on this knowing and understanding. This requires that teachers gather defensible and dependable evidence from many sources, and hold collaborative discussions with colleagues and students about this evidence, thus making the effect of their teaching visible to themselves and to others. (Hattie 2012, 19)

STRESS RELIEF: FOCUS ON IMPACT WITH THE GPS

It is important to remember that not everything can be accomplished in one year. When you consider how your school will address a big, multi-year district goal, you may feel that developing only one or two performance objectives isn't enough. But, there are a couple of things to remember. First, there is no expectation that the district goal will be accomplished in only one year. Goals are challenging to achieve. All that is expected is that your school will do its part. The second thing to remember is that your performance objectives are based upon the information gleaned from your CNA snapshot. Go back and review the prioritized problem statements. Your school's problem statements may not address everything in the district goal. That's okay. If every school addresses their prioritized problems through performance objectives, an inspection of all the POs from all schools will address all areas of the district goal.

Remember, the district uses data from your school and all other schools to develop the district goals. You should not create a performance objective in areas where your data shows no need. When all schools conscientiously address their areas of need, the district goal will be addressed.

Chapter 8

STRATEGIES

"A great strategy is born of constraint." Terry O'Reilly

My cousin, Julie, got married in a church in downtown Dallas, Texas. My mom, grandmother and I drove from New Mexico to Dallas to attend. As we were entering Dallas, my cell phone died and the charger was in a suitcase in the trunk. We no longer had a GPS, but we were confident because the invitation contained a map to the church. When we drove into downtown, what we thought would be an easy drive turned out to be more challenging. We found many one-way streets. The skyscrapers made it difficult to determine if we were driving south or west, and some street signs were impossible to read. Eventually, we did find the church.

We were happy to unload after such a long drive, taking our gifts, cameras, and anticipation with us—ready to enjoy this happy family event. We climbed the stairs in front of the large auditorium, paused to snap a couple of pictures and then entered the church. We didn't recognize anyone, but since we lived out of town, we didn't find that unusual.

As I was about to sign the guest book, a somber woman approached me and said, "Hello, I'm Carol's mother." My first thought was, "Who is Carol and what did you do with Julie?" As I was trying to decide how to respond, I happened to look inside the auditorium for the first time and where I expected to see flowers ready for a wedding, I saw a casket surrounded by a different kind of flowers. We were in the wrong church!

We were about to attend a funeral instead of a wedding, with presents and cameras in hand. We sincerely apologized and hurriedly left the church. Going down the stairs as guests were arriving for the funeral was awkward. It was very hard not to laugh at our mistake but out of respect, we were able to stay straight-faced until we were back inside the car. I learned two good lessons from this experience. First, having a goal (attending the wedding) is not enough. Not even having a performance objective of arriving on time is enough. I needed a better strategy – better actions to create efficiency and prevent veering off the path. It takes all three parts of the GPS - a goal, a performance objective and a strategy. (I needed a GPS - in more ways than one.)

The second thing I learned is to always keep my charger close and be grateful for the GPS on my phone that can take me directly to the correct address. Luckily, the correct church was just around the corner, and we walked in and sat down before the bride arrived. Knowing where you want to go—and getting to the right place—is essential when it comes to continuous improvement. Students don't have time to wait.

Strong strategies in the GPS helps schools meet current students' needs without wasting precious time and resources. It's also important to keep that GPS right out front - where it is visible to everyone. That way, the busy distractions of the day won't pull everyone off course. See Figure 8.1 for a model of the GPS with a focus on the strategies.

Figure 8.1 Strategies and the GPS

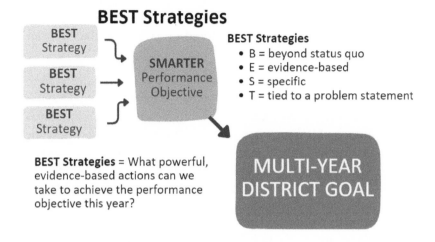

BEST Strategies

BEST Strategy	
BEST Strategy	
BEST Strategy	

SMARTER Performance Objective

BEST Strategies
- B = beyond status quo
- E = evidence-based
- S = specific
- T = tied to a problem statement

BEST Strategies = What powerful, evidence-based actions can we take to achieve the performance objective this year?

MULTI-YEAR DISTRICT GOAL

WHAT IS A STRATEGY?

A strategy is a bold and targeted action that when achieved, along with other related strategies, will help the school achieve the associated performance objective. There are typically one to three strategies per PO. That is worth repeating. Only one to three strategies. That means the strategies must be powerful because they identify the actions that are needed to achieve the PO. There is no room for actions that don't work. A good way to measure the quality of your strategies is by using the BEST acronym in Figure 8.1.

CREATE BEST STRATEGIES

Educators have a tendency to move fast when it comes to planning strategies. Just as soon as a problem is identified among a group of educators, someone jumps in and offers a solution. "I heard that the school in the next county bought the latest shiny program, and they are experiencing tremendous success. We should buy it, too, right?" Well…not so fast. Don't let the fear of missing out cloud your thinking. There are much better steps to follow if you want to implement the most successful strategies.

1. First, carefully study your problem statement until you and your team fully understand it. Then, analyze the root cause. If there is more than one root cause, you will need to address each with separate strategies. You may need to go back to the CNA for more details.

2. Now, brainstorm ideas that *might* effectively address the problem and prioritize two or three ideas to explore further. This is a time when it becomes important to have the right stakeholders present. Make sure you include those who will implement the strategy and people who may have differing perspectives. As you are working through the brainstorming process, be aware that finding the right strategy might not mean adding something new. A current strategy or resource might work well if repurposed or implemented differently. Or the strategy can also be to *stop* doing something. (See The Stop Audit in Chapter 9.)

3. Next, answer these questions for each of the two or three strategy options. Eliminate any of the strategy options that generate a "no" response to one or more of these questions:

    • We have enough time available for implementation and monitoring of this strategy option.

    • We have enough personnel to implement and monitor this strategy option. (If funding is already in place to add new personnel, you can answer this question with "yes.")

    • Funding is available to support the cost of implementation the first year and the cost needed to maintain the strategy for at least two to three more years. (Consider the cost of both people and materials.)

    • Can we confirm that this strategy option will not complicate or conflict with other strategies already being implemented or other new strategies in the CIP?

    • Can we confirm that other schools using this strategy have not reported any unintended consequences with the implementation of this strategy?

4. Research the effectiveness of the strategy options. This is where many schools' planning processes fall short. Research takes time, but it's worth it. ESSA requires strategies to be evidence-based and it is critical to use reliable sources for your research. We will explore ESSA's Tiers of Evidence and how to determine the effectiveness of a strategy later in this chapter.

WHAT GOES IN A STRATEGY?

You will find strategies written in many different ways in the GPS. Some strategies are simple and don't need as much detail as others. Some strategies are large and may even need specific action steps outlining what needs done, by whom, and when.

All strategies need these components:

- **What** will be done specifically and **by whom, when,** and **for how long?** This can be included in the strategy description if the strategy isn't very complicated. An example of a simple strategy might be to purchase a set of reading books for students to keep at home so they will not be without one in class or at home. A more complicated strategy may need actual action steps included in the strategy. An example would be if the school decides to expand tutorials to include a before-school morning option. Some of the activities might include:
  - o Revising the bus schedule
  - o Planning professional learning and planning time for the teachers
  - o Writing a letter to inform families
  - o Purchasing supplies
  - o Informing all of the staff
  - o Assigning a room

And there are probably other things that need to be done. When strategies are more complicated, like this one, it is helpful to create a numbered list of action steps. Include everything that needs to be done, assign it to someone, and add a due date.

- **Who** will be responsible and who will help monitor progress to ensure the strategy is implemented with fidelity? Be specific! Assign one or two people to the strategy. The monitor doesn't have to be the person "in charge" of the strategy. Select anyone responsible. Every quarter when it is time to hold a status check to measure progress, the person or people assigned to the strategy come to the meeting prepared to give a 1 or 2 sentence status update. Others have the opportunity to also report, but by assigning someone you can be sure that strategies don't get overlooked. Don't assign more than two people because when a group is assigned responsibility, people often think someone else is taking the lead and nothing gets accomplished.

- **How** will you know the strategy is successful and by what evidence? When you develop the strategy, think about the status checks along the way and the evaluation at the end. What does success look like? Make sure everyone is clear about what this strategy is intended to accomplish and how it will look along the way. Write the details in the strategy.

- Is **funding** required? If so, include additional details, such as the funding source, budget codes, and a description of purchases.

- Will **professional learning** be required? If so, include cost and other additional details. Does professional learning include ongoing support? How? Always consider professional learning. Remember, school improvement occurs when the behavior of adults changes. People need professional learning and support.

THE HEXAGON TOOL

Trying to figure out what strategies will work best in a school isn't easy. Every school will respond to strategies differently, even if they have the same problems and challenges in their CNA. What works really well in one school may not work at all somewhere else because students and teachers are unique. When every minute and every dollar count, not having a clear-cut plan frustrates busy educators. If this is where you are, there is hope! The Hexagon Tool can help you quickly sort through options and determine which strategies have the greatest potential for success. Developed by the National Implementation Research Network (NIRN) at the University of North Carolina at Chapel Hill, The Hexagon Tool is an exploration, discussion, and analysis tool. Its purpose is to help schools analyze the fit and feasibility of implementing new strategies *before* investing time, money and other resources.

The Hexagon Tool, shown in Figure 8.2, is best used by a team to facilitate discussion and generate diverse perspectives. It is designed around six contextual fit and feasibility factors that identify:

- Alignment with a prioritized problem in the CNA

- Fit with current initiatives

- Availability of needed resources and supports

- Validated evidence that it works and in what conditions

- Staff's confidence of success and readiness for implementation

- Capacity to implement, support and sustain

The tool can be used at any stage in a strategy's implementation, but it is most commonly used when schools are exploring new options. If you hear of success in another school, working through The Hexagon Tool is a good first step to see if the same strategy is a potential fit for your school. It can also be used after a strategy is in place to diagnose challenges related to contextual fit if that strategy isn't producing the anticipated results.

To use The Hexagon Tool, gather 5-8 people with knowledge about the problem and the potential strategy. In that group, it is helpful to have people who have diverse perspectives and 1-2 people with no direct link to the problem. The group will begin with a review of the performance objective, the prioritized problem statement, and the root cause before looking at the potential strategy.

The process is simple. Provide a copy of The Hexagon Tool and Worksheet located in Appendix H. Begin with a short overview of the potential strategy. Start with the Need factor (prioritized problem) on the Worksheet and discuss the first five questions. Then, have the group individually score each question by selecting the number (1-5) that best aligns with their view. The scores equate to 5 - strongly agree, 3 - neutral, and 1 - strongly disagree. Continue with the other five factors and after scoring each question independently, compile the group's scores and find the mean for each factor. Using the discussion notes and group's scores, the committee will complete The Hexagon Tool Form marking each of the six factors as potentially achieving high, medium, or low success if implemented. While the ratings alone should not be used to determine the final recommendations, this process can shed light into areas that otherwise might go unexplored. The tool and the questions for each component are located in Appendix H.

Figure 8.2 The NIRN Hexagon Tool

Hexagon Tool

Confirm the need was identified through a needs assessment process.

Assess how well the intervention's evidence is likely to address the identified need.

Identify if the school has the necessary capacity to support and sustain the strategy.

Establish whether expertise in the intervention is available and accessible.

Assess if the intervention fits with current initiatives, structures, and values.

Examine its fit with local, state and federal policies, priorities, and requirements.

Assess if the school feels confident that this strategy will lead to the intended outcomes.

Assess the level of buy-in for the strategy.

Identify availability of necessary resources:
• technology/data
• staffing
• training and coaching
• physical infrastructure
• administrative and system supports

Assess what additional resources are required for implementation, the potential cost, and funding.

Examine validated evidence for the intervention on what works, in what contexts, and with whom.

Assess the evidence on implementation cost.

Hexagon labels: Need, Fit, Capacity to Implement, Readiness to Implement, Resource Availability, Evidence

Strategy

The Hexagon Tool can be used to evaluate the potential of strategies as you are exploring options. Strategies are evidence-based programs and practices.

Please rate the aspects of implementation of readiness by checking the appropriate box.

	High	Med	Low
Need	☐	☐	☐
Fit	☐	☐	☐
Resource Availability	☐	☐	☐
Evidence	☐	☐	☐
Readiness to Implement	☐	☐	☐
Capacity to Implement	☐	☐	☐

ALL STRATEGIES HAVE THREE OUTCOMES

All strategies will result in one of three intended outcomes. Tony Frontier and James Rickabaugh, in their book, *Five Levers to Improve Learning* define those intended outcomes as:

1. Maintenance of the status quo

2. Transactional change

3. Transformational change (Frontier and Rickabaugh 2014, 14)

Maintaining the status quo sounds like a negative thing, but the truth is that we engage in maintaining the status quo all the time. Every year, especially at the beginning of a new school year, there are a considerable number of logistical planning needs that must get done. Some examples are enrolling students, creating the master schedule, assigning teachers to classrooms, communicating the bus schedules, preparing to write and publish monthly newsletters for families, ordering materials for classrooms, etc. Many of these activities have been implemented in previous years and are deemed to be acceptable again for the new school year. These are about effective management and clarity of tasks. Status quo strategies should not be included in the continuous improvement plan.

In transactional changes, you exchange one thing for something else. The problem with this type of change is that we often expect dramatically different or improved results. Frontier and Rickabaugh describe remodeling your kitchen (transactional) and then expecting your food to taste different (transformational). We know that doesn't make sense. But we do the same thing in schools all the time. Here are some examples of transactional changes in schools where we might expect transformational results:

*   Isolating the freshmen by moving all of their classes to the same hallway

*   Provide all students with a laptop

*   Implementing newly expanded bus routes a schedule change

*   Implementing standards-based report cards instead of traditional report cards

- Implementing ratings from a new framework for teacher evaluation

The third type of change is transformational. This type of outcome requires people to think differently. In March of 2020, the COVID pandemic caused all schools to experience a huge transformational change. Schools transformed from being in person to online. The whole concept of what it meant to teach and provide instruction became totally different. It wasn't just a modification - it was totally different. Students and their parents had to relearn what a school day looked like. Schools had to create new processes for attendance and collecting student work. Principals could no longer walk through classrooms. And, what about classes such as band, choir, and physical education? The entire system was transformed in a very short amount of time.

When considering what strategies to use to eliminate the root cause(s) of problems, it is important to consider whether it is a status quo, transactional, or transformational change. Only the transactional and transformational strategies should be included. Knowing what type of strategy you are considering takes thought. Instead of thinking "what does our school need to look like" try thinking as the result of our instructional program, "What do our students need to *be* like?" Our thinking needs to focus on the impact that we expect. Frontier and Rickabaugh offer these examples:

1. Is teacher evaluation about a transactional process designed to train principals to check boxes, dole out rewards and punishments, and fill out forms? Or is teacher evaluation a transformational opportunity to develop teachers' and principals' understanding of a shared model of effective practice as the initial step in creating systems of support that honors adults as learners on a path toward expertise in influencing student learning?

2. Is [MTSS]/Response to Intervention seen as a transactional sampling problem to determine which kid gets shuffled off to which classroom? Or is [MTSS]/Response to Intervention seen as a transformational opportunity to prioritize standards, use assessment to inform more effective teaching strategies, and empower students to develop a better understanding of themselves as learners? (2014, 149)

So, how do we use this information when considering strategies? Here are three questions adapted from Frontier and Rickabaugh's method for focusing on the outcomes we desire. See if the strategy you are considering aligns with your answers and goes deep enough to achieve your intended outcome:

1. What is the impact we are trying to achieve?

2. Does this strategy identify the changes that will have the most direct impact on student outcomes?

3. Does the change require a transactional change in process, a transformational change in thought and practice, or both? Does the strategy fully address this?

ESSA AND EVIDENCE-BASED STRATEGIES

When the Every Student Succeeds Act (ESSA) was enacted several years ago, schools began asking questions of vendors about the research behind their products. ESSA instructs schools to seek relevant, evidence-based interventions. Almost immediately, research was everywhere. Every vendor can now show the research about why their product works best. But ESSA clearly explains that not all research is acceptable, and school leaders need to be careful about accepting research from vendors on their products. Some vendors do not understand the difference in definitions between "research-based" and the tiers of evidence that ESSA requires. They will state that the interventions are proven to work because of a positive base of research. However, it is not only about how much research is available, but also *HOW* the research is conducted that is important.

A good place to begin your search to find evidence-based interventions is the What Works Clearinghouse (WWC) website located at https://ies. ed.gov/ncee/wwc/ and produced by the Institute of Education Sciences (IES). The IES is the statistics research and evaluation arm of the U.S. Department of Education. According to the website, the WWC review teams evaluate existing research on different programs, products, practices, and policies in education. They identify quality studies with trustworthy research and meaningful findings so that school leaders can find Tier 1 Strong and Tier 2 Moderate evidence under ESSA. The WWC does not rate the overall quality of interventions. Instead, it evaluates the quality of *studies* of interventions. The WWC refines its procedures and standards about every three years based on improvements that occur in education research. See Figure 8.3 below for a better understanding of ESSA's four tiers of evidence.

Figure 8.3 ESSA's Tiers of Evidence

UNDERSTANDING THE ESSA TIERS OF EVIDENCE

	TIER 1 Strong Evidence	TIER 2 Moderate Evidence	TIER 3 Promising Evidence	TIER 4 Demonstrates a Rationale
Study Design	Well-designed and implemented **experimental** study. Meets WWC standards without reservations.	Well-designed and implemented **quasi-experimental** study. Meets WWC standards with reservations.	Well-designed and implemented **correlational** study. Statistically controls for selection bias.	Well-defined **logic model** based on rigorous research.
Results of the Study	Statistically significant positive effect on a relevant outcome.	Statistically significant positive effect on a relevant outcome.	Statistically significant positive effect on a relevant outcome.	An effort to study the effects of the intervention is planned or currently under way.
Findings From Related Studies	No strong negative findings from experimental or quasi-experimental studies.	No strong negative findings from experimental or quasi-experimental studies.	No strong negative findings from experimental or quasi-experimental studies.	N/A
Sample Size & Setting	At least 350 participants. Conducted in more than one district or school.	At least 350 participants. Conducted in more than one district or school.	N/A	N/A
Match	Similar population and setting to your setting.	Similar population and setting to your setting.	N/A	N/A

Source: https://ies.ed.gov/ncee/edlabs/regions/midwest/pdf/blogs/

Notice in Figure 8.3, in the top row labeled Study Design, certain words are underlined. They reflect the research design required for each Tier. A 2017 Wallace Foundation Report titled, "School Leadership Interventions Under the Every Student Succeeds Act: Evidence Review," defines the research design like this:

1. **Tier 1 (Strong), Experimental Study** - Random assignment of participants to intervention and control groups.

2. **Tier II (Moderate), Quasi-experimental Study** - Nonrandom assignment of participants to intervention and comparison groups by (1) providing intervention to one group or (2) using existing data, identifying a comparison group of nonparticipants. Must demonstrate that the groups were equivalent before the intervention started.

3. **Tier III (Promising), Correlational Study with Controls** - Using existing data, correlations between intervention status and outcomes must control for factors related to selection bias (e.g., participant demographics, prior associated outcomes).

4. **Tier IV (Rationale), Research-Based Rationale** - Well-specified logic model that builds on high-quality prior research or a prior positive evaluation. (Herman et al. 2017, 11)

In addition to the WWC website, there are other websites to search. Two of those include the Best Evidence Encyclopedia (https://bestevidence.org) and the Evidence for ESSA (https://evidenceforessa.org) both created by Johns Hopkins University School of Education's Center for Research and Reform in Education. When considering a new strategy, it pays to do your homework. It is easy to believe that popular instructional products and strategies must have strong evidence supporting their effectiveness, but it is important to read the research yourself. You know your school's demographics and other information. Compare your school's statistics with the statistics of the schools in the research. When you analyze the research, use the Hexagon Tool, and involve the right stakeholders, you are likely to select quality, evidence-based strategies to address the needs identified in your school's CNA.

INNOVATIVE STRATEGIES BUILD ON OTHER IDEAS

Some of the brightest minds on the planet have designed highly effective, yet simple, solutions to the world's problems. How did they do it? Did they have one eureka moment that blasted all prior ideas out of the proverbial water? It's never that easy.

In his essay, "The Myth of the Sole Inventor," Mark Lemley, Stanford Law, wrote that many inventions are created simultaneously by different people. It's an incremental process where one person has an idea and develops a part. The next person builds upon that idea. "It means that it is not the first flash of an idea that is necessarily the important one; the value of an idea often comes only after various people have honed and refined it in various ways." (Lemley 2012, 7)

Lemley refers to Eli Whitney's invention of the cotton gin as an example of a process that was simply improved upon and rushed to market faster than that of his competitors. "Whitney's gin worked well, and that's worth something. But it seems that other people were developing similar ideas at around the same time." (Lemley 2012, 12) This is good news for educators. When brainstorming strategies that may help answer the problem statements that you've identified, do not be overwhelmed by the idea that innovation must come from something new. Sometimes it is looking at a solution – one you may already be implementing - through a fresh lens. Explore. Listen. Read. Learn from others. And then think about how you can do what you are already doing, but better.

One elementary school principal I interviewed shared a solution to a problem that was effective, not difficult to implement, and didn't cost the district additional funding. In fact, the solution involved looking at a problem through a different perspective.

The problem was that parents/guardians were not engaged in their child's learning journeys. This created issues with teacher communication, homework, and learning deficiencies. However, the school's Advisory Committee reviewed the data from the CNA and helped devise a different format for parent/family and teacher communication. It was so successful that the very first year it started to transform the connections that families made with the school.

Instead of the traditional parent/family-teacher conference where a family member comes in to listen to a teacher talk about the student's progress, the principal decided to create a more relaxed, relational environment that involved the students. Essentially, it was a family conference.

Students prepared for the family conference in class. They worked on their goals for the year and how they would present their current learning status to whomever the student wanted to invite. The family conference included a conversation between the teacher, family member(s), and the student. The family members were given a list of questions ahead of time to help them be prepared. A teacher might ask the family members about the child's strengths and the family's hopes and dreams for the student. The student had an opportunity to talk about strengths, challenges, goals, and areas of interest. At the end of the meeting, the teacher elaborated on the goals for the year, and together they determined how to work collaboratively to help the student reach their goals. The school offered both in person conferences and conferences through an online meeting platform. Both were a success. Before this change, parent-teacher conferences were only attended by about 80% of families. The family conferences tallied at a 93% attendance rate and received very positive feedback.

This type of authentic, two-way communication builds trust and relationships; a relational connection is critical for student growth and success. The teachers compiled the parts of the conference that did not contain confidential student information in a document that was used as data for the school's comprehensive needs assessment. As the year progressed and additional family conferences were held, the document was updated to show progress. This was a simple and innovative way to create personal relationships and engage families with their students' learning. An added benefit is that the school is able to consistently gather meaningful feedback from families as part of the continuous improvement process.

What does this story have to do with building your strategies?

First, it serves as motivation that not every strategy has to involve the purchase of a new costly program. Second, it reminds school leaders that strategies can reflect authentic work designed for continuous growth. The improvement plan is not a document that sits on a shelf until next year when it's time to update it. Finally, this innovative idea generated through the school's Advisory Committee reminds us that finding value in what we do is what drives our beliefs, and our beliefs are what drive our actions. These hearken back to a school's mission and vision.

STRESS RELIEF: AIM FOR SIMPLICITY

One word of caution when working on strategies for your GPS– keep it simple. Some schools and districts write hundreds of strategies to accomplish their many performance objectives and those are the plans that usually end up on a dusty shelf.

At 806 Technologies, when the team begins designing software, a UX designer carefully considers how the user will interact with the software. The goal is to minimize a user's cognitive load and decision-making in operating the software so that the user receives benefits from the software with little stress. If it takes too much work to use the software, the user will quit before receiving benefits. School leaders need to operate like a UX designer when creating a continuous improvement plan. If there are too many strategies, people cannot remember which ones are priorities and nothing gets done well. Fewer strategies have a stronger impact on change.

Here's why. There are a number of researchers who study working memory in humans. While they disagree on the exact amount of information that humans can hold in working memory, that number seems to fall somewhere between three and seven chunks. (Think about telephone numbers in the U.S. They are broken into three- and four-digit sections for a reason.) Author, speaker, and worldwide expert in whole system change Michael Fullan says, "When we strip away the clutter, we make change less complicated, and we get at the small number of actionable items that make a bigger difference. Change then gets easier, the speed of quality implementation accelerates, and the results are more sustainable." (Fullan 2011, 155) So, when your team begins to develop your school's GPS, it is essential for your sanity and for the effectiveness of your plan that you keep it simple.

Choose no more than two or three performance objectives per goal. When exploring how to achieve those objectives, look at three or fewer strategies per objective. It may feel wrong to leave things out because we want to fix everything all at once. But, it is wise to work smarter and better by focusing on less at one time. The Pareto principle is a useful thinking tool for helping school leaders select priorities. It states that 80% of outcomes come from 20% of causes. We need to focus on the vital few issues, problems, etc., that will have the biggest impact if addressed. Pareto's thinking keeps us from trying to be all things, for all people, in all areas, all the time. It also helps figure out where to allocate our precious resources of time, energy, and dollars in ways that will have the most likelihood for success. (Conzemius and O'Neill 2014, 241)

Chapter 9

MONITORING PROGRESS AND EVALUATING SUCCESS

> *"Monitoring the level of impact and success your work*
> *produces may be the most important action a school can*
> *take. It is no secret that we learn from doing."*
> Emil Posavac

What Posavac is saying is that the best GPS in the world will not make a difference if the implementation isn't monitored and evaluated. It will be ineffective. Monitoring progress as the plan is implemented and evaluating success at the end of the school year are two important components in the continuous improvement planning cycle. School leaders move their schools forward through influence. It's not enough to develop a plan and put it out there hoping for the best. "Leaders often complain that it takes as much effort to measure an influence campaign as it does to deploy the campaign itself. And within this complaint lies the real problem. Leaders assume measurement is completely separate from influence. It isn't. Measurement is an integral part of the change effort, and if done correctly, it informs and drives behavior." (Grenny et al. 2013, 23) Monitoring progress is critical in the continuous improvement process.

WHY MONITOR?

The goals are big, and it may seem that accomplishing them won't happen until far into the future. The POs break the timeline down into the current school year, but even that timeline can seem distant and quickly forgotten as school starts. Back-to-school activities quickly melt into football season, fall carnivals, school pictures, parent/family meetings, the holidays and before you know it, it's January. The school schedule is a beast!

When schools create their continuous improvement plans, it is always with intent to implement and achieve. But keeping focused on the strategies is difficult when so many non-strategy-related activities are occurring. That's where the power of checking progress about every 90 days is beneficial. When the continuous improvement plan is developed, three dates for status checks to measure progress are set on the calendar. Space them out about every 90 calendar days and schedule a fourth date for the end-of-year final evaluation. Mark them in red and make them non-negotiable. These meetings are critical to the school's success and should be ranked at a high level of importance. "When intent, effort, and results are aligned across a school's planning processes, the school accelerates toward a desired outcome with a level of efficiency and effectiveness that otherwise would not have been possible." (Frontier and Rickabaugh 2014, 11)

As you conduct a 90-day status check and study the strategies' progress, your team will likely notice one thing: educators are sometimes impatient and tend to look for the quickest way to finish – no matter what the task. It's difficult to get busy educators to slow down and examine their progress, but it is one of the most important aspects of continuous improvement. James Clear says it this way:

> Reflection and review enables the long-term improvement of all habits because it makes you aware of your mistakes and helps you consider possible paths for improvement. Without reflection, we can make excuses, create rationalizations, and lie to ourselves. We have no process for determining whether we are performing better or worse compared to yesterday. (Clear 2018, 244)

Status checks or progress monitoring allow educators to fine-tune their craft. Deliberately stopping to reflectively think about what is working and what isn't, helps point everyone back to what is important. It keeps the goals visible and ensures that you are working on the right things. It provides time to make course corrections and adjustments before major issues arise. Even when things are going very well, it pays to take time to examine progress and ask how a good strategy can become even better in the future. In effective schools, leaders are never satisfied with present success. There's always more that can be done.

LEARNING FROM DOING

Quarterly reviews, 90-day status checks, or progress monitoring – the title doesn't matter. What does matter is *this* is where the magic happens. Nothing is more powerful than learning from our actions. We can read about success, observe it in other schools, hear about it from other educators, but until we implement strategies ourselves, we won't know what works in *our* school with *our* students. Clarity comes from engagement, not thought. Who is better to determine what works and doesn't work than the teachers and principals working with students every day? Ninety calendar days is short enough that these school leaders won't lose focus, but it's long enough to make significant progress with the strategies in the GPS. Enough time goes by that there is evidence of success to celebrate. And the time is short enough that if something is not going well, the details of implementation are still fresh enough to examine.

Checking for progress is what teachers do every day in the classroom. A 90-day status check is the same except it is measuring progress on a larger scale. The strategies that go into the continuous improvement plan exceed the impact of one classroom. So, it takes a team of teachers and principals to create school-wide success. "The key message is that practice, especially deliberative practice, drives better practice. Practice is our best bet for finding solutions and for liberating innovation." (Fullan 2011, 155)

Sometimes teachers fear 90-day status checks and when that happens, it's time to work on the school's culture. Fear says, "I'm afraid you will judge me to be a poor teacher if your students do better than mine."

The confidence schools gain from continuous improvement says, "We know that all children are unique. We also know that not everything we try is going to work. Because we are professional educators and mission-driven colleagues, we have the skills to figure out how to help all students learn. They are not your students and my students. Regardless of which classroom they sit in, *all* of them are *our* students, and we share collective responsibility for their success."

HOW TO MONITOR

Respected education researchers, such as Rick Stiggins, John Hattie, and Robert Marzano, have reshaped school leaders' thinking to understand that the reason we implement any strategy is to alter specific actions to improve teaching and learning as quickly as possible. In "the old days," educators often used the term "ongoing" in the CIP instead of designating actual dates for status checks and a final evaluation. Identifying that a strategy was continually being implemented was deemed a success. For example, if the school provided tutorials, typically that was the only detail written in the CIP strategy box. Providing tutorials was the strategy and successful interventions were assumed to be taking place. The monitoring section of the plan just said, "ongoing." There was nothing to show how the instruction was implemented or how it impacted the students. Thank goodness, the days of developing "general strategies" without important details are gone!

In successful CIPs, strategies contain details for implementation and then more details about progress during scheduled status checks. At the end of the year, a final evaluation measures the impact the strategy has on the root cause of the problem. Remember that the prioritized problem is the content used to create the performance objective. The root cause of that prioritized problem is the content used to develop the strategy. Reviewing the progress of the strategy during a status check should produce evidence of eliminating the root cause so that the performance objective can be achieved.

How do you monitor? The 90-day status check meetings can be conducted quickly when people come to the meeting prepared. The status check meetings should be widely attended because school improvement is a collective responsibility – everyone participates. Key members of the staff bring laptops so they can document progress in the continuous improvement plan. Those members are the school's leadership team and anyone designated as a strategy implementation monitor or scribe in the continuous improvement plan.

Start the meeting with a review of the school's vision to create focus. Then, refer to the first goal and first performance objective in the continuous improvement plan. Read the first strategy. Remember that every strategy has one or two people designated as the implementation monitors – the "eyes and ears" observing the strategy's implementation. The implementation monitor orally gives a 2-3 sentence update on the current progress of the strategy.

If everything is going well and there are no questions from anyone in the room, the implementation monitor records what was said in the continuous improvement plan. Then the meeting's facilitator goes on to the second strategy and the next implementation monitor speaks. The meeting quickly progresses through the strategies with short reports from implementation monitors. If concerns come up about a strategy, the facilitator takes note of which strategy it is and skips past it to complete all other strategies. Don't stop to solve the problem now. Complete all strategy reviews first. There is a big benefit to having the implementation monitors speak about the progress of the strategies. It reminds the entire staff about what the school is trying to accomplish which helps them support those who are directly doing the work.

Save the conversation for those one or two strategies that need additional consideration to the end of the meeting. Dismiss everyone except those directly involved in the concerning strategies. Discuss the concerns to determine if they can be solved now or whether another meeting needs to be called. Do you need more information? Do different stakeholders need to be consulted? Do additional data need to be collected? Create a plan to resolve the issues and determine when to meet. When everything is settled and the needed adjustments are made to the strategies, be sure to inform the entire staff. This can be done through email, Slack, or a similar method. Be aware that if adjustments involve changes in procedures or actions for people not present, those people should be told in person and provided an opportunity for discussion so that the changes will be implemented the way they are intended.

If you find that your 90-day status check meetings are too lengthy, there are "monitoring hacks" you can implement. First, a one-page report can be given to the staff at the beginning of the 90-day status check meeting with certain strategies and their status already completed. For example, some strategies may be very narrow in focus such as a specific professional learning event. For example, the counselors may be learning new techniques to monitor and support student wellness. If they are currently going through the training and have not yet started to implement anything, this strategy can be reported on the one page sheet and then later, when they are actively implementing their new skills, the strategy's monitor will do an oral report for the staff. This doesn't make the strategy any less important. All strategies in the continuous improvement plan are based upon prioritized problems, so they are all important. But at this time, it is appropriate to save time and inform the staff of progress on paper rather than through a verbal report.

Another reason to list a strategy on the written report is that maybe the performance objective and its strategies are tied to a certain time of year, and this review isn't during that critical time. For example, the strategy may be to provide a smooth transition from middle school to high school, and it involves a summer "fish camp." In November-December, it could be appropriate to report progress in the written report.

The final reason why a strategy might be listed in the written report is that it is going exceptionally well. This is something to celebrate! But, don't skip the review. Monitoring critical process and outcome variables to verify that an effective program stays effective is a crucial activity after programs have been successfully implemented. (Linfield and Posavac 2018, 6)

THREE QUESTIONS AND A CAUTION

There are three questions that can be used in both 90-day status checks and the final evaluation. It may take slightly different wording for each circumstance, but the impact of these questions is continuous learning and moving forward. Three questions, ones that are useful to nearly any kind of debriefing:

- *What?* What have I learned about the topic that brought this group together?

- *So what?* What difference does it seem to make - for example, to my teaching or my team's planning?

- *Now what?* What steps can I take to make the most of what I have learned? (McDonald 2007, 20)

A caution for 90-day status checks and the final evaluation is that even though the days of general, ongoing strategies are gone, that old "ongoing" term still pops up sometimes. Don't let it. Maybe the strategy proceeds for a long time, but every 90 days there should be observed progress. If not, we need to question the strategy's design. A 90-day status check gives busy educators a scheduled time to stop and reflect on their practices and progress.

Principals and teachers race through each day and their jobs are never done. Often, that fast pace causes educators to do things the way they have always been done because there's no time to figure out another way. Conducting a high-quality 90-day status check with fidelity is one of the best ways to ensure that practices and procedures *do* get upgraded, strategies *do* get completed and goals *are* achieved. Even if the strategy will continue the next school year, a final evaluation at the end of the year is critical. The information gleaned about the strategy's status is essential for the needs assessment for the new year. It will also help you refine the strategy for the new year so that it continues to grow in strength. Building expertise and creating improvement doesn't happen by chance; it happens by intention.

THE FINAL EVALUATION

A strong end-of-year evaluation of the GPS in the CIP has always been the Achilles' heel for many schools. This is because district-required timelines for budgeting and planning for the next school year don't align with the school's continuous improvement planning cycle at the end of the current school year. It is difficult to build a budget for the next school year in February or March - long before you'll know if your school will meet the current year POs and successfully accomplish all of the strategies. But, many school districts start their budgeting process that early.

ESSA programs, such as Title I, require yearly evaluations and that information is critical for the comprehensive needs assessment for the upcoming new year. However, schools need their CNA much earlier than June to help them prepare for budgeting and personnel for the next school year. So, do schools conduct a CNA snapshot they will use to build the next year's GPS in February-March or do they wait until June-July or will they do it both times? It is a conundrum, but most schools opt for doing it early. That makes getting the final CIP evaluations for the current school year completed at the end of the year easier said than done.

The last few weeks of school are so busy and when the students go home for summer, families and other stakeholders become difficult to find. Teachers want time at home and don't want to return to school for evaluation meetings. Principals are tired and are scrambling to gear up for everyone to return in just a few short weeks. It is a tough time to conduct CIP final evaluations.

Additionally, there's not just one way to conduct a final, summative evaluation. There are several things to consider;

1. What is the purpose of the evaluation?

2. Who will conduct the evaluation and what are the team members' responsibilities?

3. What are the research questions?

4. How will the data be collected?

5. What is the timeline?

6. How will the findings be reported and to whom? (Dunsworth and Billings 2012, 7)

The information from a final evaluation is the first data to consider when revising the CNA snapshot for the new school year. Knowing if programs, practices, and strategies met last year's POs and how close that moves the school's progress toward reaching the bigger multi-year goals is invaluable. This gives you valid starting points to set POs for the new year with advanced strategies. Other considerations to think about:

1. Are the strategies equitable for all students and all student groups?

2. Are the strategies implemented with fidelity? Is implementation conducted the way it was intended?

3. Does the professional learning and follow-up match what is recommended?

4. Do all of the staff have a shared commitment to fully implementing the strategies?

The final evaluation can range from fairly simple to deeply complex depending on the size of the strategy and the complexity of the associated PO. Try a simple process first. A strategy or program evaluation form is included in Appendix I. If that process does not produce the desired results, try using a more thorough evaluation tool, such as the one produced by the Institute of Education Sciences (IES). It is a very detailed Program Evaluation Toolkit and can be found online at IES>REL Program Evaluation Toolkit (https://ies.ed.gov). The toolkit begins by helping you design a logic model or graphical representation of the relationship between the parts of the strategy and its expected outcomes.

It's time to step up our evaluation game and replace the "I think this is working" conversations with *real* evidence. The best way to start is by finding better ways to simplify the evaluation timelines.

ALIGN THE PLANNING TIMELINE AND CIP EVALUATION TIMELINE

To prevent the evaluation of your CIP from becoming separate from your evaluation for federal programs, such as Title I, Title II, etc., let's review the school's evaluation processes for POs and strategies and make some adjustments.

1. **Identify one or two measures that will be used to evaluate the effectiveness of the strategy.** You did this when you developed each strategy and added them to the CIP. You were probably thinking about measures for the very end of the planning cycle - the end of the school year or whenever the strategy is completed. Keep that in mind.

2. **Identify a point of comparison.** You can't demonstrate progress or change unless you've identified a point of comparison. Investigate the data that are already available at different times of the year. For example, can you use the information from the universal screener given to all students at the beginning of the year? Has that screener been in place for more than one year? Is this data relevant to the strategy? If the answer to all three questions is "yes" then use this data as a point of comparison.

3. **Determine the best time of year to record the evaluation.** Since you are already conducting 90-day strategy status checks, one of those checks can also serve as the final evaluation. The third 90-day status check might be the best choice. For example, if you need to fund a supplemental tutorial program using federal dollars, you can conduct the final evaluation during a 90-day status check in February.

The key is to use data to compare from February to February. Last year's February data serves as the baseline against which you will track performance for this year. How much academic progress did students make from the beginning of school in August to February of last year? The year before? How does that data compare with this year's growth?

You will also want to continue to monitor and document how much progress students make from February to the end of the school year so that you can ensure that growth stays on track. Evaluating data from August to February and then again from February to August for three years tells a good story about the success of the tutorials. It allows the principal and other stakeholders to make evidence-informed decisions during the budget and staffing meetings that occur in the early spring.

STRESS RELIEF: EMPOWER OTHERS

The CIP evaluation is tough when school leaders try to do this alone. One way to set the expectation that this is a team process is to create a CIP calendar at the beginning of the school year when you and your team are developing the GPS. Either put a large calendar on the wall in a common area or use an electronic format. As you and your team develop strategies for the continuous improvement plan, think about when it makes the most sense to conduct the final evaluation. Write that date on the calendar. Then work backwards and identify the date(s) for data collection and for the 90-day status checks. Add the name(s) of the people you assign to monitor the strategy to the calendar entries. Make sure they understand that strategy's timelines so that the right data and observations will be collected and documented during the appropriate 90-day status checks. The more information you can include on the calendar about the entire CIP process - the CNA, the GPS, the status checks and final evaluation - the more you are helping your school see that continuous improvement planning is "the way we conduct business at our school." Using a calendar also helps prevent busy educators from veering away from the plan.

Evaluating the strategies can show if the strategy is highly effective, effective, marginally effective or if it needs to be abandoned. Don't forget about that last option. We never want to hop from strategy to strategy, but when something isn't working, stop doing it. Clinical psychologist Dr. Henry Cloud, in his book *Necessary Endings*, says that "The same broken plan combined with greater amounts of hope will never produce a bigger impact." (Cloud 2010, p. 89) Let's get real. Hope is not a strategy, so we shouldn't keep repeating the same strategies year after year! In fact, a strategy shouldn't be repeated more than two years without some sort of adaptation or upgrade. Your evaluation can help with knowing what that should look like.

A caution here is that sometimes when determining a strategy needs to be abandoned, you're talking about a "beloved" project or program. Be sure your culture is in good shape before going down the path of strategic abandonment. Listen and acknowledge the sadness people feel when asked to stop something they love to do. Talk about it together and have them be part of the solution. Rely on the data for support. Michael Fullan says, "It seems elementary to say that change is about interaction with people, but that is exactly the essence of the matter. Have good ideas but process them, and get other ideas from those you work with, including -- no *especially* -- those you want to change. We now know that the more complex the change, the more that people with the problem must be part of the solution." (Fullan 2020, 45) School improvement is about helping people grow and sometimes that comes with pain. Use your data and good evaluation processes to lessen that pain.

Chapter 10

TRANSFORMATION – THE METAMORPHOSIS

> *"We are all a work in progress.*
> *Transformation is not an endpoint, but a process that can lead us on a*
> *positive path if we choose to learn and grow from our experiences."*
> George Couros

Why do some schools thrive and grow no matter what comes their way while other schools struggle? Knowing the answer to this question would be better than winning the lottery. There's no one answer because educating children is both an art and science and no two classrooms are ever the same. A tremendous amount of research has been done studying what works in classrooms and even the best researchers don't always agree.

It's much the same with continuous improvement planning. Look at the processes in two districts and you are likely to find differences. That is why the continuous improvement planning ideas and tools discussed in this book are presented as ideas. The ideas are tested and are currently creating success for a number of schools. But these ideas are not *the* model for school improvement. There is no single best way to organize and conduct continuous improvement planning. The hope is that the ideas presented will be a springboard to help you create or refine processes that are best for your school and your students. There are other options for continuous improvement planning that go deeper into planning. This book is designed to keep the continuous improvement planning processes as simple as possible but you may find areas where you need to dive deeper or try a different structure. It is ironic that the very thing that gives us freedom (no one single best way) is often the very thing that creates difficulties for us (But, *how* do we do it?).

A MONUMENTAL MYSTERY TRANSFORMS THINKING

There is a story found on the Internet that is frequently used to explain the Five Whys Root Cause protocol. It also shows how problems can appear to be very complex when, in truth, the solution is quite simple. The story begins with a 50 pound block of marble falling off the top of a column at the Jefferson Memorial in Washington, D.C. Thankfully, no one was hurt. The rest of the story is entertaining, and it paints a clear picture of the Five Whys protocol. Joel Gross, author of *The KaiZone*, read the story and decided to investigate to see if it is true or folklore. He found that the story is a little of both. The true story is that the "why" behind the crumbling building was a mystery. Acid rain was proposed, but it was quickly shot down by the fact that similar monuments nearby were in good shape.

A group of private consultants was hired by the National Park Service to perform a year-long study of the deterioration of both the Lincoln Memorial and the Jefferson Memorial. Ironically, just one month after they published their report with NO evidence of serious structural problems, the chunk of marble fell. That accelerated the process of seeking the root cause of the structural damage so it could be repaired. From here, the story evolves into some folklore. If you haven't heard this story, I encourage you to watch the three minute video of "The Jefferson Memorial and the Five Whys" by Jerilyn Edginton before reading the rest of this section. You can find it on YouTube at https://www.youtube.com/watch?v=qBidLFt8ZLA.

The story says that a chemist reported that the crumbling was due to the jet fuel from a nearby airport mixing with the soap that was used to wash the exterior of the building. He said the mixture caused the premature aging process of the monument. Because of this, someone suggested moving the airport. Can you believe that anyone would even consider voicing such a crazy idea? That's what the folklore says, and it makes a good story!

Obviously, that wasn't a practical solution. So, the next step was to begin asking "Why" the memorial was deteriorating.

1. Why, for example, was the staff using harsh soap to regularly wash the monument? The answer was pigeon droppings—many of them.

2. So, then why were there so many pigeons at the Jefferson Memorial? Enter another expert: the pigeon expert. He deduced that the pigeons came to the monument to eat the large number of spiders who hung out there.

3. Why were there so many spiders hanging out at the Jefferson Memorial? A spider expert determined that the spiders were there to eat the midges, which are described by *Merriam-Webster* as "tiny, dipteran flies."

4. Once again, they looked at why. Why were there so many midges at the Jefferson Memorial? Common around large bodies of water, these tiny flies have a short reproductive life. They come out of the ground at dusk and die soon after.

After asking more "whys," the committee tasked with the issue discovered that "at dusk, flood lights were turned on to light up the memorial which attracted the mating midges. There they died, falling to the ground all around the memorial and attracting spiders."

In the end, the overall conclusion was that the light attracted the midges, which attracted spiders, which attracted pigeons, which meant the memorial was covered with pigeon excrement and had to be washed with high-powered cleaning agents. This, combined with the jet fuel, created a chemical cocktail that caused disintegration of the building— which was a danger to the passersby. So, what was the solution?

Simply turning off the floodlights an hour earlier kept the midges away, so spiders did not gather to eat them, and pigeons didn't fly nearby to get to the spiders. Without pigeons making "deposits" all over the monument, there was no need to wash the monument as frequently. The premature aging of the monument slowed down and the airport remained in place. Edginton, in the online video, humorously proposed, "But it makes you wonder how many airports we've moved lately because we stopped asking *why*."

What does the Jefferson Memorial story have to do with transformation in schools? Two things. First, when big problems exist, (tourists are in danger of being hit by 50 pounds of falling marble) we typically think big solutions must be needed (move the airport). But that isn't always the case. Big problems appear to be a crisis needing swift action. Sometimes the best solution becomes visible when we slow down, ask questions, and do our research before acting. The second thing is that continuous improvement planning efforts tend to have an evolutionary character. According to Anthony Bryk:

> The evolutionary aspect of improvement work requires leaders to maintain a sense of humility as to what they really know and can do. This is a departure from the aura of invincibility that some leaders try to project, and it coincides with a recognition about improvement knowledge more generally: the guidance afforded by a working theory of improvement is provisional and always subject to change as new learnings surface. (Bryk 2020, 195)

KNOWING WHAT TO STOP

As you plan to implement new strategies for transformational change, be sure you choose what to stop to create room in the curriculum or schedule. This should be a deliberate process. Arran Hamilton, Douglas Reeves, Janet Clinton, and John Hattie in their book *Building to Impact, The 5D Implementation Playbook for Educators* say, "At an absolute minimum, we propose the RULE of TWO-for-ONE. In other words, for every ONE change initiative that you propose to start, find TWO initiatives of similar time commitment that you are going to stop." (Hamilton et al. 2022, 82) Do you know how many strategies from the past teachers are hanging on to – thinking they must do it all? Word-of-mouth expectations about what to start and stop are not enough. Here is an example of what can happen.

When I was assistant superintendent for curriculum and instruction, a parent called me to complain about a test her high school student was given in class. The parent claimed that a teacher spent two class periods showing students a fictional movie designed purely for entertainment – one of those movies that would be streamed at home on a Friday night – and the students were tested over the movie's content for a grade. I hadn't met this teacher yet; she was new to our district. So, I decided to go introduce myself and find out more.

The teacher was a young, first year teacher. I welcomed her to the district, introduced myself, and told her about my role in the district's curriculum. When I asked her about the movie, she told me she thought it was part of the district's curriculum and showed me why. She pulled a folder from a filing cabinet and said she had been instructed to find the district's curriculum there. What she showed me was actually a "catch-all" file with pieces of old curriculum, extra materials, old lesson plans, and a hodge-podge of other things.

Why the movie information was in there was a mystery. Maybe with a previous teacher, it had been a folder of personal things to keep. Regardless, we had clearly failed this new teacher. It made me sad that she had not received the onboarding support she needed to access the district's real curriculum. In a school system, leaders must be diligent about clearly communicating expectations for curriculum and instruction.

Hamilton, et al. developed a bold way to determine which strategies, or "projects" as they call them, with a four column tool called "The Stop Audit" which is listed in Figure 10.1 below and the explanation in the paragraph that follows.

Figure 10.1 The Stop Audit

ALL CURRENT PROJECTS	PROJECTS WITH SYSTEMATIC EVALUATION DATA	PROJECTS WITH STRONG AND POSITIVE VALUATION DATA	POSITIVE PROJECTS THAT STILL NEED PUMP PRIMING
List all special projects.	Narrow the list.	Narrow the list again.	Continue with these projects only.

(Hamilton et al. 2022, 84)

Here is how The Stop Audit works. In the first column on the left, list the names of all your active special projects or strategies. Copy them from column one to column two *only* if you have systematically collected and evaluated the data. "If you have not set up evaluation protocols, your project is more likely to be busywork that's not worth your time, and we recommend that you assume that anything you are NOT evaluating is having no impact." (Hamilton et al. 2022, 84)

The third column narrows the list again. Copy projects from column two to column three *if* the systematically collected evaluation data show at least moderate effects. You can determine moderate effects by finding the means of your pre- and post-assessment data. Then determine how many standard deviations lie between the two means. In education research, Cohen's d value of 0.20 is small, 0.40 is moderate and 0.80 is a large effect size.

"If your pre/post assessments don't show a gain of at least d=0.40, then consider carefully whether they are worth continuing." (Hamilton et al. 2022, 84) Finally, copy the remaining successful projects from column three to column four if they are generating impact, but still need focused support. In other words, the projects are producing results, but aren't yet able to be sustained without focus and priority. When they become strong enough to be sustained on their own or the original need goes away, they can be removed from column four. The projects or strategies in column four are the only projects you should continue.

The previous chapter stated something that is worth repeating here. School leaders must be given the authority to carefully examine the data and determine which strategies and old practices to strategically abandon. Adding more strategies without removing what isn't working is never a good idea. See Appendix I for an additional tool to evaluate the effectiveness of strategies.

BUILD YOUR CONTINUOUS IMPROVEMENT PLANNING PROCESSES

The reasons why traditional school improvement plans don't work are the foundation for how you build a successful continuous improvement planning culture. You can have the best plan in the world, but if it isn't housed within a healthy, vision-focused and mission-driven culture surrounded by sustainable, clearly defined processes and systems, it will not make a difference.

So, first let's address how leaders operate in a continuous improvement environment. Mike Myatt is recognized as an authority on leadership and an advisor to Fortune 500 CEOs. He says,

> As the world continues to evolve, so must our leadership acumen. Real leaders must learn to hack time-tested leadership principles to make them more relevant, practical, and effective. Leaders must stop holding on to false truths held as real, and lead in new and different ways. Leaders must spend more time exploring what they don't know rather than waxing eloquent about what they do know. They must seek out diverse and even dissenting opinions in search of what's right rather than being concerned about who gets the credit for being right. (Myatt 2017, September 18)

That is continuous improvement. It is about being clear about your vision – your north star – so that the barrage of noise (technological changes, cultural shifts, mental health challenges, safety concerns, teachers resigning in record numbers, etc.) doesn't move you off track. It's about having a plan, a real plan with details and processes so that you know what to do no matter what comes next. Leaders celebrate what is working with students, teachers and families and then encourage them when things get tough. It's building a culture of growth. Continuous improvement processes consider the research on the most effective practices and encourage us to think deeply about how practices might work with students. It's about testing what we think we know as well as what we don't know. Continuous improvement gives school leaders permission to bravely move forward with courage and resilience. Continuous improvement leaders are what all students deserve.

In an article published in *The Phi Delta Kappan* journal, Isobel Stevenson, director of organizational learning for the Connecticut Center for School Change, identified six essential conditions that must be present if school leaders want their plans to have a good chance of succeeding. (Stevenson 2019) Here are Stevenson's six conditions with adaptations to align with the CNA/GPS:

1. A needs assessment reveals a few priority problems with root causes.

2. Strategies address root causes and are powerful enough to reach the associated performance objective.

3. The strategies' steps are sufficiently detailed and include clear expectations (what must be done by whom) with descriptions to ensure intended implementation.

4. Professional learning required to effectively implement the strategies is clearly defined and planned.

5. Expected evidence of progress is clearly described with defined monitoring approximately every 90 days.

6. Actions are aligned and plainly articulated from the district goals all the way through what students will experience in the classroom.

Where does your plan rate with these Significant Six? Do you have processes and systems in place that support the actions needed? Author James Clear says that "Success is not a goal to reach or a finish line to cross. It is a system to improve, an endless process to refine." (Clear 2018, 252)

Since returning back to school after the COVID pandemic, there has been a lot of attention on emotional health and well-being. Rightfully so. Schools are asked to do more with less. Everyone is always in a hurry. Stress abounds. These are major reasons why it is important to have strong processes in place. With continuous improvement planning firmly in place, you can prevent scope creep or kitchen sink syndrome where things keep being added and piled on without formally being evaluated for value and necessity. Simplicity reduces stress. Schools don't want to waste resources on strategies or POs that don't produce a high impact. The most efficient strategies and performance objectives use fewer resources (time, money, personnel) and produce a high impact. If your school isn't moving forward as fast as you think it should, spend some time thinking about the performance objectives and associated strategies. Where do they fit on the Impact/Effort grid in Figure 10.2 below?

Figure 10.2 Impact Grid

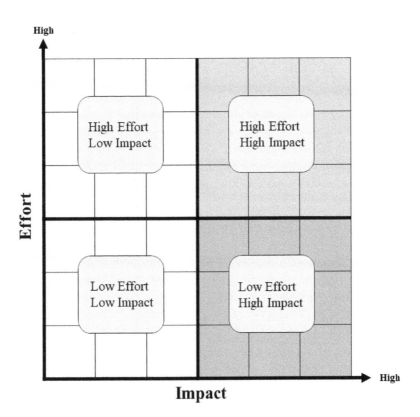

On a recent fall day, my mind was in a million places. I had a trip to pack for, important work deadlines, and my washing machine quit. So that day, when one of my nails painfully broke up to the quick, I had very little emotional margin left. So, I did what I could. I scheduled a nail appointment at my local salon.

Why am I telling you this? An experience at the salon slowed my millions of thoughts down to a more reasonable pace. A television show playing on the screen helped me realize what I was struggling with, and it's something we all struggle with at times: feeling too overwhelmed to be effective.

The television show playing at the salon was "The Joy of Painting" by Bob Ross. An American painter, Ross was famed for teaching the "everyday man" to paint via a 30-minute television show on PBS. He made a huge impact on how beginning artists thought of themselves. They led them to be able to call themselves painters. His calming voice and mantra of "happy little trees" was soothing when a student couldn't mix just the right color or figure out which stroke to use.

One thing I noted about Ross's show that afternoon was his commitment to the process. He would paint what appeared to be a rather thick stripe of purple on an otherwise lackluster canvas blocked out by a dark blue background. However, because of his commitment to the process of layering small strokes on top of small strokes, the large purple stripe became a mountain scene over top of a beautiful landscape of ocean waves.

In other words, stick with it. Be all in. In the crazy busy environment of school, stay the course. The best continuous improvement planning begins with a robust CNA and that helps your team develop a powerful GPS. With that foundation directing your focus, work the plan with intentional implementation and fidelity. Conduct status checks every 90 days to provide clarity and rebuild confidence. Change is hard and often slow. There will be bumps and naysayers along the way. Forge ahead anyway. Don't get nervous when you don't see immediate results. If you have done the right background work to ensure alignment between your problem and your strategy, keep believing and keep going. Make adjustments as needed, but don't quit too soon! You can do it and your students deserve it.

WHERE THE PEOPLE ARE

When the mission-driven people are working together toward a common purpose, and supporting each other along the way, schools experience transformation.

But make no mistake: there isn't anything magic about it.

It requires a continuous commitment to asking the right questions, finding root causes, encouraging stakeholder participation, and providing the best support systems possible. Even when everything is in place, the possibility exists for problems to arise once the plan for transformation begins to take shape. The potential for backsliding or slippage requires school leaders to reconnect, recommit and keep going. The importance of monitoring was stressed in Chapter 9. Regular status checks are the best things you can do to keep your school's progress on track. And remember– transformation doesn't happen overnight. Real progress won't happen evenly. All schools will experience "growing pains," and this is especially true with new strategies. Professional learning, coaching, and support are needed to help school leaders "unlearn" previous practices as you begin to try new methods and programs. When you are deep in the weeds of implementing strategies, it's often hard to see the other side. That's another reason why monitoring and support are so important. The ability to make mid-course corrections is essential to a strategy's success.

Even with mid-course corrections and awareness of potential problems, there can still be some backsliding. This is an implementation dip, and it can occur with a school's continuous improvement efforts just like it does with new teachers. First-year teachers begin the school year strong, but by early October, they are often very tired. The "honeymoon" of the new job wears off, and reality sets in. These new teachers begin to feel overwhelmed and sometimes even question whether they should stay in the business of teaching. This mirrors what can happen with continuous improvement planning. Michael Fullan defines the implementation dip as "the inevitable bumpiness and difficulties encountered as people learn new behaviors and beliefs." (Fullan 2011, 71) We can put a lot of time and effort into new strategies and not see any change for a while. Or, we see a small amount of change and then nothing. Fullan says that if we want to be successful and see transformational change, there are two things to remember:

1. When you are on a crucial mission, stay the course against all odds.

2. Be impressively empathetic when it comes to opposition in the early stages. (Fullan 2011, 30)

It's easy to feel confident with new strategies at the beginning. But, when you meet the implementation dip, the ground feels shaky. That's where educators sometimes get into trouble. At that point, there's no "proof" that the strategy is working, and people are starting to complain that "this is hard" so you begin hearing this little voice in your head telling you to stop everything before a big mistake happens. Fullan says no. He says that "because change is hard, all effective leaders are driven by resolute purpose with respect to deep human values. They simply do not, and would never, give up." (Fullan 2011, 30) Meet people where they are and understand that change is not fun. But if you feel confident in the CIP process that developed the strategy, stand firm. Outlast the implementation dip.

Elliot Ransom is Co-CEO of UChicago Impact, an organization that works to empower educators to use research and actionable data to improve practices. In a blog article, he writes, "It's important to remember that having high-quality data is great, but it's not enough. It's what you *do* with that data that really matters." (Ransom 2021) People hold the key. Data handed to school leaders in beautiful charts and graphs will not change anything. School leaders who understand the data and act are what is needed. If you want to solve a problem, you really have to see it and understand it. Working the continuous improvement plan matters. Action leads to better thinking. Simplify. Explore. Understand and then go!

There is a big difference between knowing what we should do in schools and getting the job done. Every school and each classroom is so different. Developing practice-based actions that work in all situations is the goal of improvement planning research. But it will never be accomplished completely. That's the beauty of working with people, and I challenge you to view that as a blessing and not a curse. Contrary to what is often reported through the media, many schools ARE growing and getting stronger. School leaders are embracing data and drawing on evidence from others working on the same problems.

Continuous improvement is a learning journey. It is an ever-evolving process. "Dwell on your own situation and practice - as well as that of other practitioners - as a basis for action. Draw continuously on outside ideas but always in relation to how they relate to your situation, and how it could be improved." (Fullan 2011, 21)

WHAT THE PEOPLE SAY

You often hear principals and teachers cry for "no more change." One thing that the pandemic in 2020 made clear is that educators can and must engage with change. We live in a rapidly changing society. A school that doesn't change will die.

Students embrace change. It's all they know. Think about the careers available to today's students that did not even exist less than a decade ago. Or technology—how rapidly it changes. In schools, many decisions are required to be made more rapidly than ever before. This is why long-range strategic plans that were popular before the COVID pandemic rarely go past three years now. Who can even guess what education will require in ten years? Or even five? Students don't care about our long-term plans. They care about today. Parents want to know that our focus is on *their* kids and not our future students or past students. At the same time, we must teach students in ways that will serve them tomorrow.

To successfully implement the continuous improvement cycle, school leaders must take the time to think through the change and make it "sticky." What will it take to give the implementation staying power? Meaningful change begins at the individual level. Change needs to focus on:

- The vision for the school
- The promises in the mission
- The core values
- A collective effort to improve learning for all students
- Deficits in the processes and not the people

- Clear, consistent communication

- Trust and eliminating the fear of failure

- Strong, dynamic relationships

STRESS RELIEF: "WE" IS ALWAYS GREATER THAN "ME"

In your pursuit of continuous improvement, remember the proverb, "It takes a village to raise a child." The same can be said for "raising" a school's success. It takes a village. The reason for having a continuous improvement culture that uses data, monitors its own impact, and works collaboratively as a team is that *everybody's* practices improve. If you've come this far, then you understand that continuous improvement is not an event and not something that can be done alone.

My grandson, Ben, played T-ball for the first time this past year. Watching 5-year-olds learn the game of baseball will bring a smile to anyone's face. When it was their turn to take the field, Ben's entire team participated. They were all over the field – multiple infielders and outfielders, and some stood in positions that I know aren't in the playbook. They picked dandelions and wore their gloves on their heads. They were so entertaining to watch. When it was my grandson's turn to bat for the first time, Ben hit the ball and took off running to first base. The entire crowd – from both teams - exploded with cheers, but as he got closer to first base, I could tell something was wrong. By the time he got to the base, he was in tears. The first base coach covered him in a big hug and asked him what was wrong. Ben was upset because people were yelling his name as he ran. He thought he was in trouble. The coach told him the crowd was cheering him on – that they were excited for him, and they were encouraging him to run faster to the base. Ben asked, "But why? They don't know me."

What Ben was saying was true. This little team had just formed and none of the boys on either team were in the same kindergarten class. The kids didn't know each other and neither did the parents. Ben's question reminded me of a quote I read in a blog post written by George Couros. The quote is from Ari Gallop, and it says, "Think about what's possible if we cheer for complete strangers." Wouldn't our world be a better place?

Back to Ben's story. The second time Ben was up to bat was completely different. He hit the ball and ran. This time, his body language was completely different as the crowd cheered. He hopped onto first base with a big grin on his face. He knew the crowd was supporting him and cheering him on.

What would happen if we cheered each other on like that? Regardless of where we work or if we know each other or not. What would happen if everyone who cares about schools celebrated the little wins and the big ones. What would that teach our students? People tell us to learn from our failures, but nobody likes to fail. Change is not easy. We are supposed to be resilient, have grit, and be life-long learners. But we get tired. Sorting through the data, trying to solve problems, and helping students grow is hard! It is hard because it is about *people improvement.*

The more we talk about it and make continuous improvement planning visible, the more it frees us from having to be right all the time. We can try new things and struggle as we learn. We can fail and not be failures. Continuous improvement becomes who we are and how we operate our school. Everybody needs a team to succeed, so now is the time to start cheering others on. With the right team and strong processes, no problem is unsolvable. You can do it and you can bet that I'm cheering you on.

APPENDICES

APPENDIX A - MULTIPLE MEASURES

**Dr. Victoria Bernhardt's
Multiple Measures of Data**

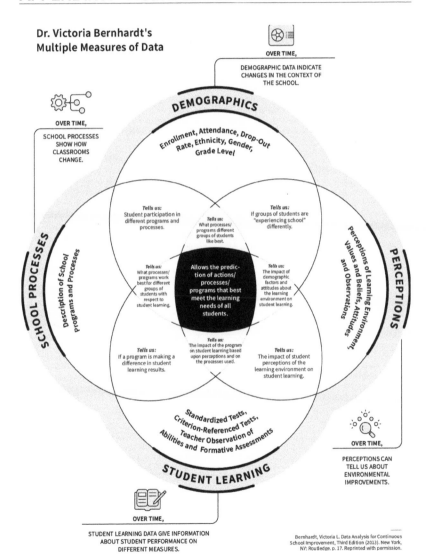

OVER TIME,

DEMOGRAPHIC DATA INDICATE
CHANGES IN THE CONTEXT OF
THE SCHOOL.

OVER TIME,

SCHOOL PROCESSES
SHOW HOW
CLASSROOMS
CHANGE.

DEMOGRAPHICS

Enrollment, Attendance, Drop-Out
Rate, Ethnicity, Gender,
Grade Level

SCHOOL PROCESSES

Description of School
programs and Processes

PERCEPTIONS

Perceptions of Learning Environment,
Values and Beliefs, Attitudes
and Observations

Tells us:
Student participation in
different programs and
processes.

Tells us:
What processes/
programs different
groups of students
like best.

Tells us:
If groups of students are
"experiencing school"
differently.

Tells us:
What processes/
programs work
best for different
groups of
students with
respect to
student learning.

Allows the predic-
tion of actions/
processes/
programs that best
meet the learning
needs of all
students.

Tells us:
The impact of
demographic
factors and
attitudes about
the learning
environment on
student learning.

Tells us:
If a program is making a
difference in student
learning results.

Tells us:
The impact of the program
on student learning based
upon perceptions and on
the processes used.

Tells us:
The impact of student
perceptions of the
learning environment on
student learning.

Standardized Tests,
Criterion-Referenced Tests,
Teacher Observation of
Abilities and Formative Assessments

STUDENT LEARNING

OVER TIME,

PERCEPTIONS CAN
TELL US ABOUT
ENVIRONMENTAL
IMPROVEMENTS.

OVER TIME,

STUDENT LEARNING DATA GIVE INFORMATION
ABOUT STUDENT PERFORMANCE ON
DIFFERENT MEASURES.

Bernhardt, Victoria L. Data Analysis for Continuous
School Improvement, Third Edition (2013). New York,
NY: Routledge. p. 17. Reprinted with permission.

APPENDIX B: DATA ANALYSIS PROTOCOL

Detail	Duration	• Limit to 60 minutes or less.
	Location & Format	• In person or online.
	Materials needed	• Data selected for analysis. • School's vision and mission statement. • Paper or online format for each data team member to record observations as a group. Use data identified previously.
	Activity purpose	• To ensure the quality of findings from the data to prevent addressing trivia • To separate true meaning from assumptions and to prevent early interpretation from preventing creative problem-solving
Steps	1. Review vision and mission	Don't skip this step. "I notice" and "I wonder" statements should be reviewed through the lens of the vision (what the school will look like when all goals are accomplished) and the mission (why the school exists and how it desires to operate).
	2. Quiet zone data review	Provide a copy of the data to be analyzed for each team member or access online. Briefly explain the key points of the data. Ask the team to sit quietly with no discussion and look for information that stands out. Ask them to write down 3-5 things that catch their attention. There are no wrong observations and they can be positive or negative. Write them as a statement beginning with these words, "I notice..." Do not include opinions, causes, or solutions.
	3. Share and compile "I notice" findings	In a round-robin order, each team member reads aloud one observation. A scribe records the "I notice" observations on a chart or computer in view of all team members. In turn, each team member reads aloud a new observation until all observations (with no duplications) have been recorded. There is no discussion. Note: Record each "I notice" statement on a new line. Number the statements to make it easier to refer to later.
	4. Quite zone data review	Next, establish a quiet time of reflection for several minutes to allow team members to study the list of "I notice" statements. On their own, each team member records 3-7 speculations or questions from the "I notice" list. These speculations attempt to offer possible explanations for the "I notice" statements or make suggestions to gather additional data or information. This is not the time to offer solutions. The intent is to gain insights into what the data suggest, how the data are connected, and what the data imply. The speculations start with words, such as "I wonder why", "I wonder how", or "I wonder if or whether..."

	5. Share and compile "I wonder" statements	Without any discussion, in round-robin order, team members read aloud one "I wonder" speculation while a scribe records. Continue until all new "I wonder" statements have been recorded with no duplications. Emphasize there are no wrong statements. Note: Record the "I wonder" statements directly across from the associated "I notice" statements. Make sure they have the same number to refer to later.
	6. Quiet zone data review	For several minutes, establish a quiet time of reflection to allow team members to study the list of "I wonder" statements.
	7. What can we control?	As a team, identify the "I wonder" statements/questions as things the school can control (inside the circle of control) and things that the school cannot control (outside the circle of control). Mark through anything that the school cannot control.
	8. Discussion and exploratory questions	Invite the team to discuss the "I notice" and "I wonder" statements that are inside the school's circle of control. Are there trends or statements that can be grouped together under one umbrella? Do some rise to the top as being more significant than others? Seek questions whose answers the team believes will reveal useful information and point in the direction of identifying learning gaps. Example: "Are we spending too much time on state assessment drills and how can we move to more effectively teaching the concepts in the standards?"
	9. List patterns and trends	Identify two or three key themes or patterns that seem to emerge and group the appropriate statements together by theme or pattern.
	10. Identify strength and problems	Highlight the positive statements in green and highlight the problem statements in yellow.
	11. Plan for additional needed data and end the meeting	Did the discussion uncover a need for more additional information? If so, what? Who will gather the data/ information for the next meeting? Set a meeting date to finalize the list of strengths and problems (needs).
	12. Next steps	At the next meeting, repeat Steps 1-10 for any new data presented. Then, use a protocol, such as multivoting, to prioritize the problems and determine how many will be addressed in the new continuous improvement plan. Next conduct a root cause analysis for each problem. The problem statements and root causes are then ready to be used to develop the GPS.

Adapted from
Venables, Daniel R. (2014) How Teachers Can Turn Data Into Action. Alexandria, VA: ASCD.

CNA Data Analysis

Data Used: ....
Date: ....
Participants: ....

I Noticed...	I wonder why... I wonder how... I wonder if or whether...
1.	1.
2.	2.
3.	3.
4.	4.
5.	5.
6.	6.
7.	7.
8.	8.
9.	9.
10.	10.

APPENDIX C – PROBLEM STATEMENT QUALITY CHECK

Problem Statement Quality Check

A problem statement is a fact that can be backed up with data. It is something that a school wants to eliminate or greatly reduce by finding the root cause(s) and developing strategies to address them.

A quality problem statement answers YES to these questions:

- ⊘ Does the problem statement focus on only one problem?
- ⊘ Is the problem verified by facts?
- ⊘ Does the problem statement provide context and details (what is the problem, who is impacted, when/where the problem occurs)?
- ⊘ Does the problem statement focus on who experiences the problem instead of who causes it?
- ⊘ Does the problem statement avoid any kind of solution?
- ⊘ Is it written in clear, jargon-free language?
- ⊘ Is it written without personal feelings or opinions?
- ⊘ Does the problem statement avoid being hurtful or disrespectful?

Example ☑ In grades 3-5, 38% of SpEd students scored at the *Meets* level on the English Language Arts (ELA) statewide assessment.

Example ☑ Advanced coursework records, grades, and CTE participation indicate that at least 52% of English Learners/Emergent Bilinguals in grades 9-12 are not meeting college and career readiness standards.

Non-Example ☒ SpEd students are not meeting expectations on the ELA statewide assessment.

Non-Example ☒ English Learners/Emergent Bilinguals are performing below their peers due to not attending tutorials.

APPENDIX D - THE FIVE WHYS

The Five Whys is a simple brainstorming tool designed to help a team find the root cause of a problem. This protocol may not be the best option for complex problems, but it helps a team dig down and consider reasons that move beyond the obvious.

Start by stating a problem and then work through the chart. Keep asking "why?" in response to each answer, which is a contributing cause. If you get to a point where the contributing cause is out of the school's control, back up one step and change the contributing cause to something the school CAN control.

The Five Whys

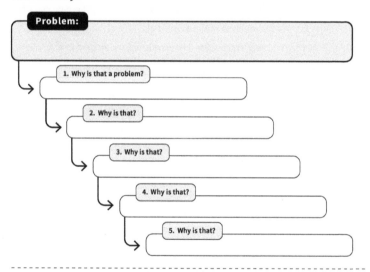

Problem:

1. Why is that a problem?
2. Why is that?
3. Why is that?
4. Why is that?
5. Why is that?

Five times is not absolute. Keep going until you can agree that you have reached the root cause, or it does not make sense to ask why again.

Helpful tips:

1. Most problems have more than one root cause. You may need to repeat The Five Whys if you have additional contributing causes that are unrelated to this first group.

2. The root cause cannot be a person. The root cause should reflect a system, process, practice, program, training, etc.

3. The University of Maryland's Root Cause Analysis Facilitator's Guide, recommends asking these additional questions to confirm that you have identified a root cause and not a contributing cause:

   a. Would the problem have occurred if the cause had not been present?

   b. Will the same problem happen again if the cause is corrected?

   c. Will correction of the cause lead to similar events?

   d. If the answers to a, b, and c are all "no" then you have a root cause. If any of the three questions are "yes" you have a contributing cause. (University of Maryland 2019, 12)

REFERENCE

University of Maryland. 2019. "Root Cause Analysis: Facilitator Guide." Accessed April 2020. https://aefb8617-015a-45da-8070-5c1c1ca5df3c.filesusr.com/ugd/514ff2_cd147deac39a410f977e3365b6290a74.pdf.

APPENDIX E - THE DIAL ROOT CAUSE(S) TOOL

Check the DIAL: From Problem to Root Cause

Identify a problem you want to solve. (Note a "we need statement.) Use data, the 5 Whys or other tools to answer the following.

Problem:

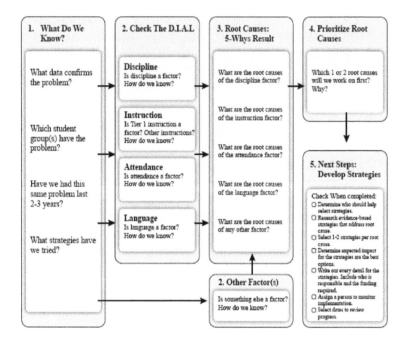

APPENDIX F – MULTI-VOTING TO PRIORITIZE

Multi-Voting to Prioritize

Multi-voting is a method for prioritizing and narrowing lists of ideas when there are too many. It's a useful method that enables teams to:

1. Create focus by prioritizing problems and root cause(s).
2. Determine which goals are most worthy of pursuit.
3. Decide which strategies are most worthy of implementation.

Materials Needed:	1. Chart tablet pages large enough for text to be seen by the group when posted on the wall. 2. Tape to hang the chart(s) on the wall. 3. A marker to record ideas on the chart tablet. 4. Sticky dots in three colors. Each person could need as many as eight sticky dots in each color.

Instructions:	1. When you announce the meeting time and place, let the team know that they will be prioritizing the problem statements/root causes and then will be identifying strategies. These can be separate meetings, if desired.
	2. You can group the problem statements by goal or list them all together. Remember that you want no more than three problem statements per goal and that three for every goal is probably too many.
	3. Discuss the list, clarifying the problem statements and defining each root cause until all questions are answered.
	4. Distribute sticky dots to the group. Each dot represents a vote and the sticky dots must all be the same color. Determine how many votes each person will receive by dividing the number of problem statements on the chart by three (rounding up to a whole number, if needed). For example, if there are twelve items on the list, every person gets four sticky dots.
	5. Have people place their dots next to the problem statements that they believe must be addressed first. Votes can be distributed one per problem statement or can be loaded up (that is, any individual can place two or more of their dots on one problem statement.)
	6. Refine the list by eliminating any problem statements that received no votes or significantly fewer votes.
	7. If the list has more than three or four problem statements, repeat the process. Divide the number of problem statements on the list by three to determine how many sticky dots each person receives for this second round of voting. For the second vote, the sticky dots must be a different color than the first vote.
	8. If, after three votes, the list of problem statements still remains too large, nominate from the floor and elect an ad hoc committee by secret ballot to narrow the final list to a manageable number.
	9. Other ways to use this process:
	  a. Prioritize which root cause to address first, if multiple causes exist.
	  b. After brainstorming strategies, determine which ones to implement.
	  c. Narrow the number of goals if too many exist. This would be done first, before working on the problems/root causes.

(Conzemius and O'Neill 2014, 118–119)

APPENDIX G - SOAR PROCESS FOR GOAL SETTING

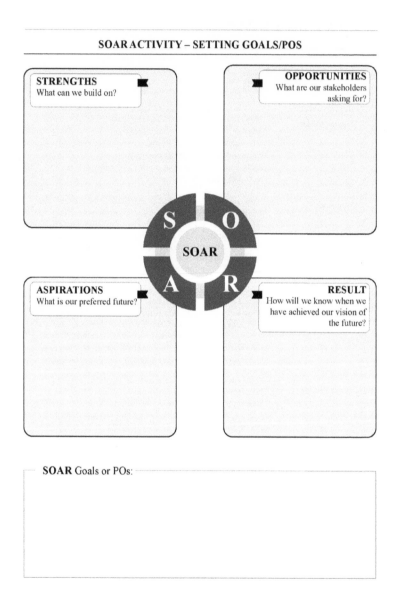

SOAR ACTIVITY – SETTING GOALS/POS

STRENGTHS
What can we build on?

OPPORTUNITIES
What are our stakeholders asking for?

ASPIRATIONS
What is our preferred future?

RESULT
How will we know when we have achieved our vision of the future?

S O A R

SOAR

SOAR Goals or POs:

APPENDIX H - THE HEXAGON TOOL AND WORKSHEET

Purpose:

To help a school team arrive at a decision on whether to select a strategy (program, process, or initiative) for implementation.

Directions:

1. Gather 5-8 people with knowledge about the need and the potential strategy. In that group, it is helpful to have people who have diverse perspectives and 1-2 with no direct link to the need.

2. Provide a copy of this Hexagon Tool and Worksheet for each participant.

    a. Review the performance objective, the prioritized problem statement, and the root cause aligned with this potential strategy. Ensure the group knows what problem you are trying to solve with this strategy.

    b. Conduct a short overview of the potential strategy.

    c. Review the diagram of the Hexagon Tool. Then go to the Guiding Questions Worksheet and begin with Need. Discuss the five questions as a group.

    d. Ask participants to individually rate each question on a scale of 1 – 5, where 1 is Strongly Disagree, 3 is Neutral and 5 is Highly Agree.

    e. Complete the other five factors the same way. Each participant will then calculate their average score for each factor.

    f. Each participant records his/her averages on the Hexagon Tool Scorecard. The group will calculate the mean score for each factor.

    g. The decision to implement or not should not be solely based upon the scoring. The discussion and insights gained during this activity should help the group determine its next step.

Hexagon Tool

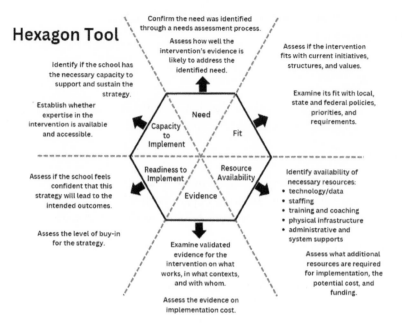

Confirm the need was identified through a needs assessment process.

Assess how well the intervention's evidence is likely to address the identified need.

Assess if the intervention fits with current initiatives, structures, and values.

Identify if the school has the necessary capacity to support and sustain the strategy.

Examine its fit with local, state and federal policies, priorities, and requirements.

Establish whether expertise in the intervention is available and accessible.

Need

Capacity to Implement

Fit

Readiness to Implement

Resource Availability

Evidence

Assess if the school feels confident that this strategy will lead to the intended outcomes.

Identify availability of necessary resources:
- technology/data
- staffing
- training and coaching
- physical infrastructure
- administrative and system supports

Assess the level of buy-in for the strategy.

Examine validated evidence for the intervention on what works, in what contexts, and with whom.

Assess what additional resources are required for implementation, the potential cost, and funding.

Assess the evidence on implementation cost.

Hexagon Tool Guiding Questions Worksheet

NEED	RATE 1-5*	NOTES
1. Is there data (e.g., student outcomes) in the needs assessment that identifies and prioritizes this specific area of need?		
2. Is there evidence that the strategy under consideration addresses a root cause or the root cause of the identified need?		
3. Is there evidence that the strategy addresses the grade level(s) of need?		
4. Is there evidence that the strategy addresses the needs of all learners?		
5. Is there evidence that the strategy strengthens core instruction?		
My Total Score		
FIT		
1. How well does the strategy fit with the skills of the staff?		
2. How likely are implementation and outcomes of this strategy to be enhanced or diminished as a result of interactions with other existing initiatives or strategies? (List as enhanced or diminished.)		
3. How does this strategy align with the school's vision, mission, and culture?		

4.	How does this strategy align with the school's and community's values, including equity and the values of diverse culture groups?		
5.	How does this strategy align with the local, state, and federal policies, requirements, and priorities?		
	My Total Score		
RESOURCE AVAILABILITY			
1.	Are there curricula and other resources related to the strategy readily available? If so, list the publisher and/or links.		
2.	If training and/or purchases must be made, what are the costs?		
3.	If the strategy requires hardware, do we currently have the capacity to support it without additional purchases? List the details, including additional costs.		
4.	Are staffing resources available for this strategy?		
5.	Are trainers available (on our staff or in the district) for this strategy?		
6.	Are coaching resources available (on our staff or in the district) for this strategy?		
	My Total Score		

EVIDENCE		
1. Is there data that demonstrates the effectiveness of this strategy? If so, where is it documented?		
2. Does data exist that demonstrates its effectiveness for a population like our target population?		
3. How much positive change is expected in outcomes with this strategy?		
4. Is this strategy rated as ESSA Tier 1 Strong Evidence of Effectiveness or ESSA Tier 2 Moderate Evidence of Effectiveness? If yes, list the URL where the evidence is located.		
My Total Score		
READINESS to IMPLEMENT		
1. Does our staff feel motivated to adopt this strategy?		
2. Does our leadership feel motivated to support this strategy?		
3. Do our staff and leadership see that this strategy will lead to the intended outcomes?		
4. Does our staff feel confident that the school can support them as they implement this strategy?		
My Total Score		

CAPACITY to IMPLEMENT		
1. Does our staff meet the minimum qualifications needed for this strategy?		
2. Does our school need to develop new or adjust existing policies and procedures to support this strategy?		
3. Does our school have a well-established partnership that can support this strategy? Is it internal or external? (Use N/A, if not applicable.)		
4. Do we have a well-established communication system that can be used to facilitate communication with internal and external stakeholders for this strategy?		
My Total Score		

* 1-Strongly Disagree, 3-Neutral, 5-Strongly Agree

Adapted from the National Implementation Research Network (NIRN) Hexagon Tool by the Centre of Effective Services, and printed with permission from NIRN.

HEXAGON GROUP SCORECARD

Factors	1	2	3	4	5	6	7	8	MEAN	H M L
Need										
Fit										
Resource Availability										
Evidence										
Readiness to Implement										
Capacity to Implement										

Give each participant a number (1-8) and list their average scores in a column. Then, determine the mean for each factor and rank it as High, Medium or Low.

APPENDIX I – STRATEGY EVALUATION TOOL

Strategy Evaluation Tool

Use this evaluation tool for program, process, or initiative evaluation. After completion, if you are unable to determine whether to continue or strategically abandon the strategy, your next step is to use a more thorough evaluation tool, such as the IES>REL Program Evaluation Toolkit (located at ies.ed.gov).

Need or Problem Statement and Root Cause

Strategy Selected to Eliminate the Problem and Root Cause

If already operational, how long has the strategy been in use?

WHY IMPLEMENT THIS STRATEGY?		DESCRIBE REQUIREMENTS AND EXPECTED RESULTS	DESCRIBE CURRENT RESULTS
Resources	If you have these resources in place, (people, materials, technology, time, funding, facilities)		Effectiveness of resources:
Activities	And you do these things, (training, support, coaching, policy/procedures, hiring, strategy)		Fidelity of implementation:
Outputs/ Evidence	You will generate these outputs, (what is produced or evidence of implementation – achievement, numbers, artifacts)		The outputs or evidence:
Value/ Outcomes	Attain this value, (effectiveness attributed to program/ initiative – changes in skills, knowledge, attitudes, behaviors, and practices)`		The outcomes or value:
Transformation	And achieve these transformational changes. (Ultimate value or effectiveness – systemic changes, sustained changes, student growth)		The achieved transformational changes:

ADDITIONAL CONSIDERATIONS	PLEASE STATE "YES" OR "NO" and DESCRIBE THE RESULTS
1. The cost-to-benefit ratio and number served is justifiable.	
2. The program/initiative can be sustained over time.	

3. There are no unintended consequences resulting from implementation.	
4. The strategy supports the school's teaching/learning priorities.	
5. The loss of the strategy will cause the need or problem to return.	

BASED UPON THESE CURRENT RESULTS, THE EVALUATION TEAM AGREES TO:

☐ Continue the Strategy   ☐ Strategically Abandon the Strategy

EVALUATION DATE:

Month/ Date/ Year

EVALUATION TEAM: PRINTED NAME, SIGNATURE and ROLE

Printed Name	Signature	Role

REFERENCES

Barth, Roland. (2002) "The Culture Builder." *Educational Leadership* 59: 6-11.

Bernhardt, Victoria L. (2017). *Measuring What We Do in Schools. How to Know if What We are Doing is Making a Difference.* Alexandria, VA: Association for Supervision and Curriculum Development.

Bryk, Anthony S., Louis M. Gomez, Alicia Grunow, and Paul G. LeMahieu. (2015). *Learning to Improve. How America's Schools Can Get Better at Getting Better.* Cambridge, MA: Harvard Education Press.

Clear, James. (2018). *Atomic Habits.* New York: Penguin Random House.

Cloud, Henry. (2010). *Necessary Endings. The Employees, Businesses, and Relationships That All of Us Have to Give Up In Order to Move Forward.* New York, NY: HarperCollins Publishers.

Conzemius, Anne, and Jan O'Neill. (2014). *The Handbook for SMART School Teams. Revitalizing Best Practices for Collaboration.* Second edition. Bloomington, IN: National Educational Service; Solution Tree Press.

Csikszentmihalyi, Mihaly. (2008). *Finding Flow. The Psychology of Engagement with Everyday Life.* 1st edition. New York, NY: BasicBooks (MasterMinds).

Datnow, Amanda, and Vicki Park. (2014). *Data-Driven Leadership.* San Francisco, CA: Jossey-Bass.

Design Thinking. n.d. "User Experience: The Beginner's Guide." Interaction Design Foundation. Accessed on July 5, 2021.

https://www.interaction-design.org/courses/user-experience-the-beginner-s-guide.

Dockterman, David. (2017). "Turning High Expectations Into Success. How Do We Actually Achieve Those Ambitious Goals We Set At the Start of Every School Year?" Harvard Graduate School for Education. Accessed on May 5, 2021. https://www.gse.harvard.edu/news/uk/17/08/turning-high-expectations-success.

Donohoo, Jenni, and Steven Katz. (2020). *Quality Implementation. Leveraging Collective Efficacy to Make "What Works" Actually Work.* Thousand Oaks, CA: Corwin Press.

Duarte, Nancy. (2019). *Data Story. Explain Data and Inspire Action Through Story.* Second printing. Oakton, VA: Ideapress Publishing.

Dunsworth, Mardale, and Dawn Billings. (2012). *Effective Program Evaluation.* Bloomington, IN: Solution Tree Press.

Forbes, Malcolm. n.d. "Malcolm Forbes > Quotes > Quotable Quote." Goodreads. Accessed June 5, 2023. https://www.goodreads.com/quotes/74883-it-s-so-much-easier-to-suggest-solutions-when-you-don-t.

Frontier, Tony, and James Rickabaugh. (2014). *Five Levers to ImproveLearning. How to Prioritize for Powerful Results in Your School.* Alexandria, VA: Association for Supervision and Curriculum Development.

Fullan, Michael. (2011). *Change Leader. Learning to Do What Matters Most.* 1st edition. San Francisco, CA: Jossey-Bass/Wiley.

Fullan, Michael. (2020). *Leading in a Culture of Change.* 2nd edition. San Francisco, CA: Jossey-Bass.

Gandhi, Mahatma. (1958). *The Collected Works of Mahatma Gandhi.* New Delhi: Publications Division, Ministry of Information and Broadcasting, Govt. of India.

Gerzon, Nancy, and Sarah Guckenburg. (2015). "Toolkit for a Workshop on Building a Culture of Data Use." Institute of Education

Sciences. Accessed on March 24, 2023. https://ies.ed.gov/ncee/rel/regions/northeast/pdf/REL_2015063.pdf.

Geurin, David G. (2017). *Future Driven. Will Your Students Thrive in an Unpredictable World?* Bolivar, MO: David G. Geurin.

Grenny, Joseph, Kerry Patterson, David Maxfield, Ron McMillan, and Al Switzler. (2013). *Influencer. The New Science of Leading Change.* 2nd edition. New York, NY: McGraw-Hill Education.

Gross, Joel. (2014). "5 Whys Folklore: The Truth Behind a Monumental Mystery." The KaiZone blog. Accessed on August 28, 2023. https://thekaizone.com/2014/08/5-whys-folklore-the-truth-behind-a-monumental-mystery/ .

Hamilton, Arran, Douglas B. Reeves, Janet M. Clinton, and John Hattie. (2022). *Building to Impact. The 5D Implementation Playbook for Educators.* 1st edition. Thousand Oaks, CA: Corwin.

Hamilton, Connie, Joseph Jones, and T.J. Vari. (2023). *7 Mindshifts for School Leaders. Finding New Ways to Think About Old Problems.* 1st edition. Thousand Oaks, CA: Corwin.

Hattie, John. (2012). *Visible Learning for Teachers: Maximizing Impact on Learning.* New York, NY: Routledge.

Herman, Rebecca, Susan M. Gates, Aziza Arifkhanova, Mark Barrett, Andriy Bega, Emilio R. Chavez-Herrerias, Eugeniu Han, Mark Harris, Katya Migacheva, Rachel Ross, Jennifer T. Leschitz, Stephani L. Wrabel. (2017). "School Leadership Interventions Under the Every Student Succeeds Act: Evidence Review." The Wallace Foundation. Accessed on December 1, 2023. https://wallacefoundation.org/report/school-leadership-interventions-under-every-student-succeeds-act-evidence-review-updated-and.

Holcomb, Edie L. (2012). *Data dynamics. Aligning Teacher Team, School, and District Efforts.* Bloomington, IN: Solution Tree Press.

Jackson, Phil. n.d. "Phil Jackson > Quotes > Quotable Quote." Goodreads. Accessed June 14, 2023. https://www.goodreads.com/quotes/527132.

Jackson, Robyn. (2023). "Is Your School Stuck in the 'Comfort Zone?'" May 3, 2023. School Leadership Reimagined. Mp3 podcast 36:46. Accessed June 7, 2023. https://https://schoolleadershipreimagined. libsyn.com/is-your-school-stuck-in-the-comfort-zone.

Kane, Elisabeth, Natalie Hoff, Ana Cathcart, Allie Heifner, Shir Palmon, and Reece L. Peterson. (2016). "School Climate & Culture." February 2016. Strategy Brief. University of Nebraska-Lincoln. Accessed on October 23, 2022. https://k12engagement.unl.edu/ strategy-briefs/School%20Climate%20&%20Culture%202-6-16%20.pdf.

Lemley, Mark A. (2012). "The Myth of the Sole Inventor." Stanford Public Law Working Paper No. 1856610. 110 Michigan Law Review 709. Updated on April 28, 2020. Accessed on June 17, 2023. https://ssrn.com/abstract=1856610.

Linfield, Kenneth J. and Emil Posavac. (2018). *Program Evaluation. Methods and Case Studies.* 9th edition. London: Routledge.

McDonald, Joseph P. (2007). *The Power of Protocols. An Educator's Guide to Better Practic*e. 2nd edition. New York, NY: Teachers College Press.

Mills, James. (2021). "Why You Need More Than School Improvement Plan Goals: 5 Critical Strategies Missing from Most Plans and How a Systems Approach Increases Ownership Beyond the Principal." Learning Sciences International blog. Accessed on November 11, 2022. https://www.learningsciences.com/blog/ school-improvement-plan-goals/.

Myatt, Mike. n.d. "Vision vs. Mission." N2growth blog. Accessed on July 18, 2022. https://www.n2growth.com/vision-vs-mission/.

Myatt, Mike. (2017). "Speeding Change By Slowing Down." N2growth blog. September 18, 2017. Accessed on July 18, 2022. https:// www.n2growth.com/speeding-change-by-slowing-down/.

Obiero, Aloo Denish. n.d. "Aloo Denish Obiero > Quotes > Quotable Quote." Goodreads. Accessed November 4, 2023. https://www.

goodreads.com/quotes/11911060-vision-sees-the-stars-mission-carves-the-path-to-reach.

Paradies, Mark. (2019). "Definition of a Root Cause." TapRoot Root Cause Analysis blog. Accessed on November 12, 2022. https://www.taproot.com/root-cause-definition/.

Preuss, Paul G. (2003). *School Leader's Guide to Root Cause Analysis. Using Data to Dissolve Problems.* Larchmont, NY: Eye on Education.

Prince William County Public Schools. n.d. "Vision, Mission, and Values." Accessed on September 15, 2022. https://www.pwcs.edu/about_us/strategic_plan/values__vision__and_mission.

Prosper Independent School District. n.d. "2022-2023 District Improvement Plan." Accessed on September 15, 2022. https://www.prosper-isd.net/Page/3378.

Ransom, Elliott. (2021). "Why Success Depends on Having the Right Mix of Data - and How You Use It." Teach. Learn. Grow. The Education Blog. Accessed on November 13, 2023. https://www.nwea.org/blog/2021/why-success-depends-on-having-the-right-mix-of-data-and-how-you-use-it/.

Reeves, Douglas B. (2021). *Deep Change Leadership. A Model for Renewing and Strengthening Schools and Districts.* Bloomington, IN: Solution Tree Press.

Sagor, Richard. (1992). *How to Conduct Collaborative Action Research.* Alexandria, VA: Association for Supervision and Curriculum Development.

School District of Pickens County. n.d. "Vision and Mission." Accessed on September 15, 2022. https://www.pickens.k12.sc.us/page/vision-and-mission.

Stevenson, Isobel. (2019). "An Improvement Plan is Not Enough - You Need a Strategy." *The Phi Delta Kappan* 100 (6), pp. 60–64. Accessed on June 6, 2023. https://doi.org/10.1177/0031721719834031.

University of Maryland. (2019). *"Root Cause Analysis Facilitator*

Guide." Accessed on November 15, 2022. https://marylandpublicschools.org/stateboard/Documents/02262019/TabG-SupportingSchoolImprovement.pdf.

Venables, Daniel R. (2014). *How Teachers Can Turn Data Into Action.* Alexandria, VA: Association for Supervision and Curriculum Development.

White, Stephen, and Raymond L. Smith. (2010). *School Improvement for the Next Generation.* Bloomington, IN: Solution Tree Press.

INDEX